IN BETWEEN THE LINES
OF FAITH AND WORK

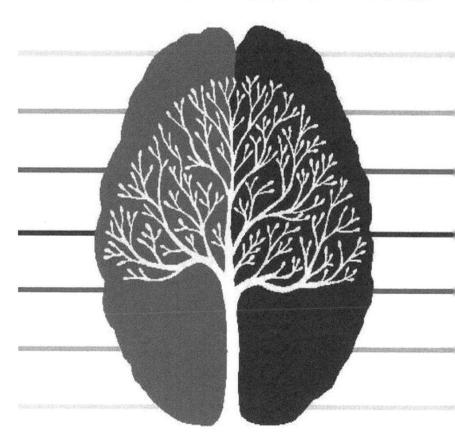

DR. ASHLEY TAURIAC

Copyright © 2018 Ashley Tauriac

All rights reserved. No portions of this book may be reproduced, stored in a retrieval system, or transmitted in any form or by any means- electronic, mechanical, photocopy, recording, scanning, or other- except for brief quotations in critical articles- without the prior written permission of the publisher.

Published in Nashville, Tennessee.

All scripture quotations are taken from The Holy Bible, English Standard Version unless otherwise stated. ESV® Text Edition: 2016. Copyright © 2001 by Crossway Bibles, a publishing ministry of Good News Publishers.

ISBN: 978-0-692-11631-9

All rights reserved.

Cover art designed by Justin Mueller.

Dedication Page

To Andy, Alyssa, Marquicia, and MJ

I can't thank you guys enough. You put in so much time, encouragement, faith, and fun into our life group. It was always such a joy and honor to work with each of you. I assume you never thought your time would eventually translate into a book (I sure didn't!), but it wouldn't exist without each one of you. Thank you for being great friends and helping me get through my training and finding my calling.

To Pastor Jerry

Thanks for randomly asking us to lead that Bible study so many years ago. You were my first friend in Nashville, and walked me through the hardest days of med school, the lowest times during my illness, and the best opportunities to serve in Nashville and abroad. Thank you for always watching out for me, and for helping me become who I am today.

To the Misfits

Thanks for being great friends and giving me a reason to keep fighting—no matter what.

Table of Contents

Introduction

I shoved the book down on the coffee table in front of me, exasperated. It skidded off the table and crashed to the ground. I left it there untouched for hours while I fumed about it.

Had that author actually attended graduate school? If so, I don't know what kind of bogus training he had gotten, but none of those suggestions were going to fly in my world. This was already my second year and it was perfectly clear I did not have the capacity to follow those rules.

I don't remember where I came across the book, but I had just finished perusing their steps on "succeeding and still keeping your faith as a Christian in graduate school." *Every single recommendation was ridiculous.*

"*Attend all church services and Bible studies.*" I tried, but I actually had school group meetings, and overnight call on Sundays, and literally couldn't go to some of the services.

"*Spend more time each day reading your Bible than you do in reading for your studies.*" Well, I have class from 8-5, then study for 4-6 hours or so... how many hours do you actually think are in the day?

"*Make sure you sleep eight hours every night.*" I didn't even do that during college before I got into medical school!

If that author actually attended graduate school, obviously they were just much smarter than I was, because if I followed their plan—I was going to fail. That wasn't *my* plan! I wanted to work hard to become an excellent doctor! *But I also wanted to remain an excellent Christian...and I started to worry I might not be able to do both.*

When I was in medical school, I occasionally served with the college ministry at my church. There were a few of us already in grad school, or in the workplace. One year the pastor asked if we older students could lead a Bible study. They were going to be traveling a lot that summer, and wanted to keep something going for the students who stayed in town. I agreed to help out, not realizing it would change my life for the next decade.

The three of us in charge of the Bible study soon discovered that the only people remaining for the "college ministry" were not in college. Our Bible study that summer consisted of several graduate students and young professionals who had just graduated. We started off the first week talking about some general Christian concepts and expecting it to be like every other Bible study we had done.

What we didn't account for was 1) we were all good friends, 2) we had all been through multiple studies before, and 3) we were all in a place in life where we needed something different than the familiar. So instead of sharing cute, happy stories about examples of faith and grace, **we got really honest really quickly about how hard life in the real world was becoming.**

"I worked for weeks on a project and did all the work. But my classmate managed to come in at the end and take credit for pretty much everything. This teacher was supposed to write me a recommendation for my internship, but now he doesn't trust me. What do I do?"

"I spent all of college being at the top of my class. It was easy for me to be the best and still have a life. Now that I'm in graduate school, I am barely passing, even though I spend every waking hour studying. I don't know how to fix it."

"My co-workers are awesome, but they're also super crude and catty. They keep inviting me out to places I would never go. But then if I don't go, they make fun of me and call me a prude. I have to work with these people all day, every day. How do I handle this?"

Honest questions about things we never thought of before kept rolling in all summer. The other leaders and I tried to find studies and books on the topics we were addressing. But the answers were either completely outlandish, like the book I described above, or they concentrated on one specific aspect of the workplace, like money, and nothing else. Even those books were far and few between.

So instead of staying frustrated, we started writing lessons from our own experiences. We reached out to other people in the church who worked non-pastoral jobs. We read books about any related topic we could find. We changed our Bible study to deal with, and delve into those difficult topics that often were not discussed.

The Bible study has evolved over the years. The other leaders and the participants have come and gone—but I'm still here, fleshing out what I have not totally mastered, but love to explore... *the fact that there is a way **to live out our career as Christians**. There is a way to learn how to treat our jobs as our mission field—as God's will and blessing and opportunity for our lives.*

More than anything, God cares about, and helps us navigate through the crazy, unknown, gray areas that our workplaces bring into our lives.

This book is about having the courage to step out and take a chance *in between the lines of faith and work.*

This book highlights my own long, twisted journey of how I learned to walk *in between the lines*. I've written about many things that tripped me up and almost took me out, in the hopes that you would be able to walk around them more easily. I pray you take your time as we walk through my rough lows, fun testimonies, and thoughtful questions. I encourage you to ask God to give you clarity and heart for the work He wants you to do.

The church cannot be the church if everyone that knows God is hiding within its walls! We can't change things without both the pastors *and the workforce* being anointed, encouraged, and ready to fight. Some were meant to shepherd and teach other Christians, *while others are meant to create, alter, and minister to the world.*

So, what is it that God has called you to?

Can you see your destiny clearly laid out before you? Or maybe you have glimpses of what you hope will come to pass? Maybe you only know where God has you in this moment, and are waiting expectantly for the next step of your life to come into view? Either way, God has called you to greatness.

God calls us to more than we can dream; once we begin walking and trusting in Him, He can take the smallest divots of time, energy, dedication, or talent we give and explode them into miracles of power. God has a plan perfectly engineered for you in your life, both in this moment and in those to come. Don't get discouraged. Don't give up. Great is your reward, not only in heaven, but also every day that you wake up and say- *forget the unknown, forget the fear, forget the struggle, forget the limitations, forget the past!*

God help me, and make me into who you've called me to be.

Changing Our Thinking

Lord of All

"The word kyrios is used to translate the name of the Lord
6814 times in the Greek Old Testament."
~Wayne Grudem

"I should strategize, plan, and organize well, but even my
best plans mean nothing unless God shows up."
~Banning Liebscher

I had a plan. I had a dream, I knew the steps to get there, and nothing was going to get in my way. It was a very good plan, if I do say so myself. My goal as a teenager was to become a doctor, and there were going to be no modifications. I was going to go to college with no distractions, then I was going to get into a good medical school and become a doctor. There were other ideas—something about a rock star, maybe a teacher, getting married, hopefully—but nothing else mattered as much as becoming a doctor.

I knew what I wanted, and I knew I had to work for it. In high school I studied hard, picked the right extracurricular activities, volunteered, and scheduled myself to death, so that I could get into a good college. And finally, I was there—at one of the best in the country—Vanderbilt University. I was starting actual pre-medical classes and things were finally starting to fall into place.

Except for my life—which kind of seemed to be falling apart. I would run around like a crazy person all day—taking six classes my first year, so I could finish all of college, pre-medical, my majors, and my music minor requirements before graduation. I was only a month in, and had already signed up for several volunteer and shadowing opportunities. A friend asked me one time, "What do you do for fun?" I couldn't answer the question, because I literally didn't understand it! There was no fun here—there were sacrifices that were going to get me to where I wanted to be! So, basically, I ran non-stop every day from 8 am to 10 pm.

But I had a little secret no one knew. Every night I would go back to my dorm room, and cry. Cry—because no matter how hard I worked, I still couldn't get it all done. Cry—because I felt so alone and so lost, even though I thought I knew what I wanted. Cry—because if the point of life was to work like a dog I wasn't sure it was worth it. And for the first time in several years, I had reached the end of my ability to work harder and figure it out. I finally started praying to God to help me fix my crazy life.

The madness had actually started back in high school, and I wasn't even sure why. I kept flashing back to awful memories—how hard I had worked, and how little it had panned out:

I smiled in spite of the tears forming at the corners of my eyes. A fake smile, but convincing once I added an empathetic, "Oh, of course. No problem, it's okay," to my friend. I walked quickly out of the room and tried to compose myself. I had to go back to class soon, and I didn't have time to lament things right now.

But it seemed I never had time to lament anything. This year—my senior year—more than anything, I was growing increasingly aware of how busy and just plain sad my life was. What was I doing all of this for? Theoretically, I was working diligently so that I could get a scholarship for college. And amazingly enough, that's what I had just been voted out of receiving.

Did they know how hard I had been working these last four years? I should have been the obvious choice—straight A's even in AP classes earning me over a 4.0, and salutatorian of the class. I used to cry if I got a 96 on an easy test in high school—if I wasn't near perfect, I considered it failing. Not to mention all of the work I had done after class— I actually had so many extracurricular activities that they didn't all fit on the applications. I should have been the perfect choice for the scholarship!

And yet I still didn't get it. Didn't get acknowledged, or get the money, or the vote for the most likely to succeed... and as the list of things that I should have earned and somehow lost grew, I was growing increasingly depressed. Why was I working so hard only to end up with nothing? I never went to one party in high school, never went on one date, spent most Saturday nights studying, or practicing, or memorizing lines for a play...but I couldn't stop. And suddenly, I couldn't win either.

And then standing in front of my entire class giving the graduation speech, I was hit with incredible sadness. I had worked like a dog for four years straight. And even though I got into a great school, I felt like I had nothing to show for it. I decided I needed to slow my pace when I got to college, and life would be fine.

But then I got to a top university with some of the smartest kids in the country, and the only way I could keep up was to study relentlessly. Whereas in high school, I didn't think once about how hard I worked, *it was all I could think about in college.* Was there no other way to live?

During my freshman year, I got connected with a campus ministry and they taught me about something I hadn't learned growing up in church—*lordship.* I knew about Jesus as our Savior—as the one who died for our sins, so that we could have a relationship with God. That part I understood completely, but lordship was way different. Basically, lordship meant that God was in charge of our lives. After believing in Jesus, the next step was placing our trust and our direction in His hands. When the Bible talked about how love is a sacrifice, and understanding the sacrifices God had made for us, lordship was the logical response back to Him. *But logical doesn't mean easy.* Many people accept Jesus as savior because they want to be saved from hell and sin—but not everyone wants a Lord in the process. At the end of the day, most people just want to do what they want to do!

Lordship sounded both positive and negative to me. On the one hand, it meant that God would take care of me—so I could stop striving, and let Him maintain the details. On the other hand, I knew lots of stories about God, and usually "trusting Him" didn't end well for the planners like me. "Trusting Him" ended with Jonah getting swallowed by a fish, until he finally relented—to give a "the end is coming" speech to people who God saved anyway (Jonah 1:17, 3:1-10). "Trusting Him" ended with pastor after pastor giving the testimony about how they wanted to pursue something, but God told them *no* and sent them to Africa or into full-time ministry! "Trusting Him," in my opinion, would end with God dragging you through places you didn't want to go, so you would learn some lesson, and then finally relent- to go in a completely different direction than what you wanted.

**Making Him Lord of my life likely meant
I was going to have to give up
my perfect plan—and I wanted none of that.**

So, it was many months before I relented—but I finally did. I put everything on the table. I imagined holding all my dreams, my expectations, and my abilities in my hands—and handing them to God. He could toss them out entirely, or He could give them back to me wholeheartedly, but He was in charge of everything I did, from that time on. It was not easy, but I committed to trust Him more than my own strategies—no matter what.

I braced myself for the coming ridiculousness—I was sure I was going to have to leave college. I knew becoming a doctor was going out the door, because anyone who truly followed God had to go into full time ministry, one way or another. Obviously, what else matters to God besides getting people saved? But a semester passed. And then another. And then another. And instead of telling me to leave my dreams behind, God was giving me permission to do what I had dreamed for years—suggesting *He needed me to be me*—more than He needed me working in a church. I realized for the first time ever, that God knows and cares for each of us personally. I started to trust Him even more.

Good and Perfect Leadership

I spent much of my life thinking that God simply wanted me to behave. To be a good girl. But in spite of my unyielding work ethic, years of denial, and determination to do it my way—God just waited patiently until I was ready to do it His way—then embraced me in a beautiful surprise when I did. Lordship is not nearly as scary as I made it out to be. But the only reason it's not scary is because of Who we are serving.

I did a Bible study over several months with my life group about *royalty*, and how we should see ourselves as princes and princesses, and not servants of God. However, it wasn't until the last week that I asked what they thought of the concept. I laughed at my thoughtlessness as they admitted they had no desire to be royalty. They started talking about bad examples of leaders we see all the time in media; and I realized how hard it is to trust anyone, when bad leadership is so common.

Thankfully, God is not just anyone. He is not an angry, possessive leader who will lash out at our imperfections. He is not a self-absorbed control freak who wants everything His own way, to the detriment of everyone else. He is not an absent, careless God who doesn't care about the things that matter to you. He is not a slave driver, determined to continue forward unendingly in his pursuits.

Thankfully, He is not you and me.

He is the already established King of Kings and Lord of Lords, and needs nothing else to add to His title. He is the all-loving Father, and the protective, encouraging confidant. He is the sacrificing friend who walked where we walk, and knows exactly what we go through. He is the world creator who gave us the ingenuity and ability to rule like Him. He literally needs nothing from us—and yet offers us everything. Putting that Person as Lord of your life is not terrifying and crazy. It's more like putting on a glove that fits perfectly, and realizing that the glove gives you powers to save the world... (Or use your own analogy, I think I've been watching too many Marvel movies lately!)

So I finally "got" lordship. I was good with whatever God wanted me to do—I trusted Him and I knew He was going to work things out well for me. I was in a really good place for a while—and then a series of unfortunate events followed. In summary, life took me out. It almost killed my faith, and then eventually my career. As I started to rebuild, I kept reminding myself of all the things that God had promised me in the past, and all the things He promises in the Bible. But when I compared the promises to my actual life I kept winding up short.

One thing that years of education *will* teach you is *delayed gratification*. You sacrifice quite a bit now and one day you will be rewarded for the things you gave up. *However,*

I got to the end of all of my training and ended up with nothing. I mean that literally—I couldn't even get a job. We are all living in the same world—where doctors are usually a hot commodity, but I couldn't find a job to save my life. And I got mad at God—what about all the things He promised? What about the payoff for all the years and time and energy I had put into school and my faith?

Thankfully, God gently and patiently pointed me back to reality. The truth is, I had made lordship about trusting God now, because of what I thought was coming at the end—all the things I felt I deserved.

But lordship isn't about trusting God because of what you are going to get, it's trusting God, even when you don't get what you wanted.

It's trusting that He's still a good Lord, even if you end up with nothing. It's placing Him firmly in charge, no matter what the ending is—knowing your true payoff comes from the joy and satisfaction of a life with God. It's *in between the lines* of what you believed for, and what God promised, that God shows up.

Not everyone hits rock bottom like I did, but everyone is faced in life with making the decision to do it their way or God's way. There are big decisions—like when God asks you to do something different then you intended. But there are also small ones—the daily decisions to die to yourself, and to believe in Someone else. To trust Someone else's thoughts, Someone else's goals, Someone else's plan. Making that decision is the beginning of true freedom!

19

Further Questions for Study:

1) Have you ever felt like truly trusting God requires you to work in full-time ministry?
   Where do you think this assumption comes from?

2) Have you given full lordship of your career to God?
   If so, how has that changed things?
   If not, what would it take for you to make that decision?

3) What is one decision in your life right now where it is difficult for you to trust God's way, instead of your own?

Mission of God

"The gospel is giving people hope that real transformation is possible."
~Sam Aiyedogbon

"True godliness does not turn men out of the world, but enables them to live better in it,
and excites their endeavors to mend it."
~William Penn

So eventually I came to better understand the lordship of God… again and again and again. To be fair, I assume I will be learning to do things God's way and not my way for the rest of my life. But life was less stressful, and God gave me the freedom to pursue incredible surprises outside of my plan.

But as I continued through college and my medical training, many questions started to arise about life. I couldn't stomach the injustice I was seeing—all the treatments that didn't work, the irrationality of the health care system, and the broken parts of life that weren't fixed by me telling someone about God. How do you send a child home with dad, knowing the child will likely be beaten and require medical assistance again; but all you have to offer for now is "God loves you?" How does that help the two-hour-old baby who is choking to death because he literally does not have lungs? How do you watch a 16-year-old with recurrent metastatic cancer cry all day from literal pain despite the best medicines, and all you have to offer is a hope *after* she dies? And if hope after death is all I have to offer, what is the point of life itself? If the goal is that we believe and pray a prayer, why didn't God set it up so that when we get saved, we immediately go to heaven? With all the pain, and all the suffering, and all the struggle that life brings here on earth, what is the point of our actual life?

I struggled a lot with this during residency. I started taking a new Bible study class with Pastor Bruce Fidler—a pastor at our church who said he loved teaching professionals because he treasured studying the mission of God. I didn't know what the big deal was- God's mission is to get people saved, right? But as we studied the message of the Bible instead of just individual passages it became very clear—God had much more in mind than simple encouragement and each of us praying a prayer of forgiveness.

God had a very clear pattern of total redemption that played out through scripture, and every time he gave the instructions again, His plan was laid out in more detail.

We started with Genesis. God created the world and said it was good. He also created man and woman and then gave them what is known as the Creation Mandate. In Genesis 2:15, God said they were to "work and take care of" the Garden of Eden. These words are of the same etymology as the words "worship and obey," meaning the way this passage was understood early on, was that our work and care of the world glorifies God. His original mandate in Genesis 1:28 told us to explore and learn about the world, cultivate and develop it, and teach what we knew to the rest of the earth.

However, after the fall, sin affected our relationships with God, with other humans, with work, and with the earth. The fall of humankind means that the original design of the world was broken. Because we rejected His authority, everything about the world—our hearts, emotions, bodies, our relationships to others, and our relationship to nature itself stopped working as it should. God had a plan for redemption—there would be a punishment in the form of sacrifices for our sins, and God would accept that for now to redeem our relationship with Him. The Earth was also now cursed, but that didn't mean it wasn't redeemable; but largely, humanity as a whole moved forward not doing everything quite as planned.

So, God initiated a Covenant with Abraham that echoed back to the one given in the Garden. In Genesis chapters 12-22, God gives more blessings, along with precise instructions for Abraham's descendants. They would care for the land, plan for offspring, be a fruitful nation, and expound to other nations. However, the Israelites were eventually enslaved by Egypt, and spent years crying out to God for salvation.

So incredibly enough, another person is chosen to lead—Moses is called and given a specific set of instructions for the Israelites—for the people they will be, and the work they will do. Once again, the covenant is given with more clarity: Israel would become a kingdom of priests—a group of teachers who were to follow God's plans, and then teach those things to the rest of the world. This is essentially the same thing that Adam was called to do, and the very thing that Jesus would be called to do one day as well. However, Israel at this

point doesn't just need a new place to live and the chains off
their back—they need true healing from the crazy, slave-
minded attitudes they have lived under for hundreds of years.
So, redemption this time was not just a new job. This time,
they needed literal social, political, and economic freedom
from the Egyptians. They needed spiritual cleansing from
polytheism and bondage. They needed emotional freedom
from human suffering and physical oppression. They didn't
just need their sins forgiven—they needed independence from
their literal captivity to be part of the redemption story. And
that's part of why the story of the Israelites being freed from
Pharaoh is so amazing. Exodus became a template for how
God would deliver in the future.

**This time, God wasn't just looking to right their
standing with Him after sin entered the world. God
was looking to right their standing with the world.**

Because once the Israelites were given their land and
new mandates, they included much more detail. There were
rules, of course, to keep people in order (Commandments and
the Law). But even more than that—they were a promise. The
laws God set out to rule were going to give them a country to
live where idolatry, injustice, and immorality that had plagued
them in Egypt were outlined as the major sins to avoid. But
the laws given were not just about what to do "at church" or
even "in their spare time," the laws were all-encompassing
descriptions of how the people should live their lives, work
their jobs, and love their communities. This would be known
as *shalom*—a word translated not just as *peace*, but as
wholeness and health of all human life.

Sadly, the laws were given to the Israelites for reasons they weren't anticipating. God knew they wouldn't be perfectly followed and used the commandments to teach us something much bigger—we can't do it on our own.

We cannot follow the rules, redeem the earth, or get free from sin without Him.

Thankfully, He had another plan and His name was Jesus. The ultimate redeemer came to Earth as the son of God. He was the perfect sacrifice to finally take care of our sins for good. He was an incredible teacher, righting much of the confusion that the people had stumbled on in the laws. He was the Healer, turning our expectations on health and sin and death. He called out injustice and division. He worked with the forgotten, the forlorn, and the ignored. He challenged the need for war that the Israelites demanded and instead preached forgiveness, and refocused on a completely different thing—lives and cultures changed and redeemed in a way that humans had never seen and never done before.

He changed everything. Then He left, and that's the end of the story, right? Wrong!!

First off, Jesus didn't just leave or die when he was crucified. He was resurrected from the dead, and in doing so, proved something else entirely—there is nothing in this world that God cannot overcome. There is no problem, no hurdle, and no fate that cannot be redeemed by God. He gave us the ability to overcome our own personal sins and those limiting the world in one fell swoop.

And second, he didn't just leave us with a bunch of unfinished problems. I skipped two main sections of the Bible! 1) The promises of the prophets and 2) The creation of the church.

Part of the reason why Jews have had a hard time believing that Jesus was the Messiah was that the prophets gave multiple promises in the grueling years before Jesus came. Similar to when the Israelites were enslaved by the Egyptians, the people were believing for more than just a Savior from their sins. *They were praying for a World Changer.* The Prophets reminded Israel of their sins and their need to put God first in their lives. Once lordship was decided, they promised many blessings. They promised God would do a new work and create a new covenant with his people. They promised changes spiritually, economically, socially, and morally—that God would gather Israel, cleanse them, and return their land. But they also promised changes that would echo across the world. They vowed for the coming subduing of God's enemies, the out-pouring of God's spirit on everyone, the renewal of Creation, and judgment; rewarding the good and punishing the evil. The Prophets left many expecting that all of this would come through the Messiah.

But Jesus came. And then left. And Israel was still scattered and torn. Evil still in charge. And the world still broken and bruised.

Instead of Jesus doing all of these things in one fell moment, he lit up a fire that will continue to burn and spread until the day He returns, and makes it all official and done. And, instead of doing all that work himself, he passed that torch to the Church. The Church would become the hands and feet of the work Jesus started here on Earth. We would work with the Holy Spirit, Who had come to us when Jesus left, to do the very things He had done. We would disciple and evangelize those around us and spread the good news of what Jesus started; the completed redemption of our sins. We would live holy lives and our work would be worship once again. We would be a voice and a teacher to take this to the rest of the world. And lastly, we would declare a holistic mission that pointed to God's coming kingdom in all human endeavors. This would be shalom and involved things such as: evangelism, holiness, sexual purity, relational health, personal development, social justice, political action, cultural development, artistic expression, earth stewardship, scientific inquiry, technological development, and much, much more.

The church would basically work with God to change the world.

We would use the gifts God has given each of us to take back the ground that evil has stolen in our lives, in our fields, in our cultures, in our nations, and replace it with the all-encompassing redemption of Jesus Christ. We would take the fire Jesus left us and set flame to the death, pain, suffering, and sin that claims far too much of our lives, and watch Him use us to play out the prophecies given long ago. And Jesus would eventually return, not to a broken, death-filled world, but to a life-giving, world-changing church.

Would your life, your job, your world, look different if you believed and lived it out like this? I have to be honest with you—I was floored when I heard the Bible laid out as a repeating story of redemption. But suddenly, I wasn't confused as to why God had let me go into medicine. If God simply wanted people saved, then really every Christian should leave their field and become a full-time minister, because let's be honest—there are a lot of people out there, and not nearly as many pastors and missionaries! But if God's plan was that the church work as Jesus did- redeeming the things around it, changing the way things were done, and teaching this to the people around us- then maybe there was a reason I had gone into medicine. Maybe God actually wanted me to use my career to help restore the world.

I love the mission of God because it made me realize that it is not a lesser calling to be in the workforce. The person who cleans the scalpels or faxes paperwork doesn't always seem like a directly important job, but the job is crucial to get everything done. And the same is true for us in the marketplace. I had a purpose to work in medicine. Maybe it wasn't to get overwhelmed and frustrated at the pain and death that plague us all. Maybe it was to look in my Bible and think about how Jesus would have changed it. Maybe it was to redeem the people and complexities I had seen in my field. Maybe it was to help others find their niche—be it business plans with integrity, or leading in historical studies, or serving where no one else would. How much different would my life be if I stopped separating work and church, and let God take over my mind, my plans, my options, my knowledge, my strategies, my thoughts—and inject what could have been forgotten with the same power that performed miracles and raised Jesus from the dead?

Far too often, our churches have sat around, scared at what they see in the culture, instead of getting fired up and ready to change it. Far too often, we sit simply twiddling our thumbs waiting for Jesus to return again, instead of using the gifts He gave us to believe for more. Far too often, our graduate students and our young professionals either leave the church or think their only contribution is a tithe. But I write all of this in the hopes that you will refuse to shrink back into the shadows. That you would believe your studies, your dreams, your learning was not just so you could watch the world take over your field, but so that you could have the opportunity to dream for God to redeem it. That you would believe there is one dream, one project, one possibility, one person, or one action that God gave you—to start a change in your field that cannot be undone. That our ultimate goal would be that the church be so filled and blessed itself, that it can't help but bubble up and spill into the lives, the culture, and the world surrounding it. What could God do with a church like that?

As a random example, I love the movie *Sister Act*. It's a cute story about a singer who accidentally sees a murder and needs to go into witness protection, so she gets placed in a convent pretending to be a nun. Let's just say, she is not very nun-like. But I love the movie because she takes the initiative to break down the walls that exist between the community and the church. In a few simple steps, the convent is befriending and serving the community where before there had been nothing in common. But just that willingness to serve speaks mountains to people who are then able to hear the gospel truth, because they have been loved and accepted by the church itself. Far too often, we sit in the midst of, but completely segregated from, the very people that need our love, our support, our encouragement, and our faith the most.

But what I love even more about the movie is the line of redemption. The choir takes literal pop songs that have no purpose in the church, but instead of throwing them out as worthless, they transform them into something that worships God. My favorite song in the movie is "I Will Follow Him," and though it is a fun pop song, it really does give you goosebumps when you watch the nuns praising the Lord with these beautiful lyrics. Those lyrics were meant for something different, but were redeemed back to our original focus as Christians—to serve, and honor, and love God.

This doesn't mean I hope to see secular songs at your church next week, but it is a great example of redemption. And that's what God gives us the ability to do in our own lives. To take our broken, crazy jobs with their sometimes warped goals and methods, and to redeem them into something beautiful. To take the broken relationships in our lives and show them what true love really is. To take that which seemed so lost and so unsavable, just like you probably were back in the day, and create brand new life, and purpose, and value. That's exactly what Jesus did for us, and exactly what we now get to do for the world. That is a mission of God worth getting on board with.

Further Questions for Review:

1) Do you think that your career fits in with the mission of God?

2) Think through some frustrations you have in your field. What does your field do with them?

3) For those problems, (major cheesy throwback coming) "what would Jesus do" in that situation?

Power Shortage

"I have learned that success is to be measured not so much by the position that one has reached in life as by the obstacles which he has overcome while trying to succeed."
~ *Booker T. Washington*

"God doesn't call us to do hard stuff. He calls us to do impossible stuff."
~*Priscilla Shirer*

So, the Mission of God calls you and the church to basically change the world. Sounds easy, right? But of course, He didn't call you without equipping you to do so. That can come in a variety of ways, but I think the one we need to focus on most is through the Holy Spirit.

Have you ever really thought about favor? Some of you probably have, and others maybe haven't. Mostly, people who have been on the wrong side of favor have thought about it before. But those who are blessed—I wonder if they always see it.

One of my favorite examples of favor is a story of an American Idol contestant. I used to watch the show a lot, and somewhere around season "fifty" or so, there was a young woman trying out who had also sung the year before. The judges recognized her, and were very excited to see her back again. But before she started to audition they interrupted her asking, "Where is your brother?" Both she and her brother had tried out the year before, but she explained that he was not trying out this year.

But for some reason, that was not good enough for the judges. They badgered her about her brother for a while—insisting that he must be in the building and she had to go find him. When she begrudgingly went to get her brother, he walked in confused. He was a tall, lanky boy with spiky blond hair who humbly waved to them and tried to leave, but the judges begged him to sing for them.

He answered the same, "I'm not here to audition, I'm just here to support my sister." But the judges wouldn't have it and begged him to sing. He got a ticket to the next round in Hollywood as soon as he finished singing. And several months later—he placed top seven on American Idol. This amazingly blessed contestant's name? Colton Dixon. He went on to score several recording contracts in Christian music and I saw him perform with Toby Mac.

Obvious favor, right? He just "happened" to be in the right place at the right time and was literally begged to be on the show—you can't pay for that incredible of a story! But I've thought about this a ton since I watched that episode. I loved that God showed up and blessed him in that moment like that. It looks like a moment of complete fortune—we all wish we had incredible favor like that!

But I imagine it didn't feel like total favor to him. I imagine the auditions the year before—he rehearsed, planned the songs, the keys, probably even his outfits! He likely put in hours getting ready for the vocal challenges required for the show. He had probably dreamed of singing in front of millions and having them appreciate his art. He was there, and positioned, and ready to win. But suddenly, he was cut and sent home.

From the Idol camera you never see all the sacrifices people made to get there. Now, I don't know Colton and haven't asked him about any of this, but listening to his songs, I am guessing the loss was hard on him. And there are a whole lot of ways that that year between auditions could have gone really wrong. He could have denounced faith in God. He could have quit music entirely. But since he was there and able to audition that day with his sister, I know he didn't. On some level, he kept plowing, kept working, kept hoping for more. And I almost love that he lost the first time around, because then it made it a literal miracle for him to get through the second time, when he wasn't even trying. Because this time, he wasn't getting in based on his work, he got in based on God's favor.

We love to see favor in our lives, but often hate to be put in the circumstances that allow that favor to develop.

But it's *in between the lines* of what you hoped for, and what you worked for, that God really moves. Sometimes it's not in the timing that we want, or expect, but He still does. When you take your dedication to your craft and God's miracle-working hands, that's when things truly become amazing. If you make it all about your dedication, you miss out on a ton of the Holy Spirit's favor. But when you trust God and do your part, things get somewhere good. And then you not only have a great outcome, but also an incredible testimony.

Favor Working Circumstances

Near the end of college, I went to a Christian conference that changed my view of working in the marketplace. My favorite sermon was called "power shortage." It was a sermon detailing that far too often we try to live our life and do our work completely in our own strength. But the pastor contrasted that with the anointing, the ability, and the favor that the Holy Spirit can bring to your place of work. I actually got a copy of this sermon and listen to it at least once a year, to remind myself that my work can be much greater than just what I bring to it, if I trust in God to make it even greater.

Jesus promised that when he left the world, the Holy Spirit would come upon the disciples and they would receive power and become God's witnesses (Acts 1:8). That same promise is true today. People normally associate the Holy Spirit with the miraculous healings of the New Testament apostles. But the first time the Holy Spirit is actually mentioned in Scripture was not related to a "spiritual calling" at all.

In Exodus, The Lord spoke to Moses and anointed Bezalel with the Spirit of God. Bezalel was not sent to be a missionary or a pastor or a priest, he was anointed to do his regular job. Exodus 31:3 says "And I have filled him with the Spirit of God, with ability and intelligence, with knowledge and all craftsmanship..." Bezalel was an artist who was given extraordinary, God-given anointing to be even greater where he was already gifted. What's incredible to me is that God would care about the excellence of the job I do every day. God has a much bigger plan of us reaching the culture as well as people's hearts. And thankfully, He isn't going to leave us alone to do so.

We can usually think of pastors who are anointed to preach, or missionaries anointed to heal or evangelize. We often attribute God's supernatural ability and favor to those who work in the church. What if the same anointing that God has given to your favorite pastor came on you to help you teach, innovate, influence, build, and redeem the very place God has called you to work every single day?

"We need anointed Christian professionals in every part of society who can call forth something incredible that the world has never seen before."

I don't remember learning much about the Holy Spirit as a child, but in studying Him as an adult I've been truly amazed at the versatility of gifts He gives.

- ❖ He is a wedge and foundation of truth.
- ❖ He is a counselor and a comforter of hearts and lives.
- ❖ He is a bold speaker who gives us words to say.

❖ He teaches us and helps us recall things we have learned.
❖ He reveals God to us even more.
❖ He gives us power to tell others about God.
❖ He leads us wisely and boldly as sons and daughters of God.
❖ He gives us new identity and strength.
❖ He helps protect what we have been given.
❖ He gives wisdom, faith, and discernment.

Who saw things in that list that might be a helpful gift to have along in their own workplace?

Just as our own lives need instruction and correction from God, our workplaces do as well. We often set out with the intent to do great things but run into problems because of our own limitations and sinful nature. Sometimes the church is often so busy copying the rest of the world, that we forget God is the one who created it all and the only one with the power to truly change things.

We first need to believe that God can and wants to anoint us to go into our workplace with Holy Spirit power. Holy Spirit power is not a pretend superpower, not a five-hour energy drink, and not a cool trick. He is a constant wireless outlet connection to the source of it all—God. The Bible details incredible people like Esther, Daniel, and Joseph who stood against "the way things had to be" and changed the entire face of cultures. It reminds me that we can pray all day long that things be different, or we can pray and take God to the place of difficulty, and let Him use us to change it.

**"What would it take for you to live beyond
your ability
every single day in your workplace?"**

Miracles Require Impossibilities

One thing we want to keep in mind when we are hoping to see miracles, is that God will often put us in miracle-requiring circumstances. Like our story of Colton above—it looks like obvious favor because he was given grace in an impossible situation. If that isn't clear, I mean that often the only way we give glory to God and not to ourselves, is when God puts us in hard places where we have no ability of our own left. That's not meant to scare you, that's just to get you in the right frame of mind. Favor for me meant getting seriously ill. Sadly, that is where I began my medical career.

After college, I finished medical school on track and was ready to tackle the last part of my training known as residency. The term "residency" derives from the word "resident." It literally meant that doctors would live at the hospital in order to fully learn their craft. So, even though strict rules have been made about how many hours residents can work, we all appreciate that we will work many long days and nights to become a stand-up physician. As I started residency, work hour restrictions were set at 80-hrs-a-wk (meaning I averaged 90 hrs.), with "q4 call" most months (meaning every 4 nights I worked an all-night 30-hour shift).

We all graduated from medical school, took a few weeks off to get ramped up, and were ready to go.

At least, that was the plan. For me, it did not go that way at all. Four days after graduation I was admitted to the hospital with bacterial meningitis and pneumonia. Meningitis is an infection of the coverings of your brain and can be deadly, so I was very blessed when I walked out of the hospital two weeks later. I was told to enjoy my last week off before residency started, and everything should be fine.

But I had this fear in the back of my mind that I couldn't seem to shake. To be fair, I couldn't actually remember graduating from medical school, and only believed it when people showed me pictures of myself there. So how could I remember everything I learned in medical school? I could barely sit up long enough to eat a meal, let alone run around a hospital for a thirty-hour shift. And though most people associate doctors with confidence and poise, I was having a hard time spelling my own name. But, being the hard-working overachiever I am, I went to work anyway— ready to take it slow and do my best. I prayed God would bless my work. He had called me to medicine, surely, He would fix everything anyway!

Three days later I was working in the always hectic Emergency Room. I examined a vomiting patient and did an exam. I gave a plan of action, listened to the family tell a funny joke, and then walked out the door chuckling to myself. At least, that's what I assumed I did. As the door shut and I finished laughing, my mind went blank. I could not remember anything— whether or not the child was critically ill or what had happened. I always wrote notes, but this set of notes was completely different. The paper had a list of impossible numbers (like vomited 500 times), incorrect spellings, and trailed off into a list of random letters and even shapes that are not in the alphabet and have no meaning at all.

Tears welled up in my eyes that I had to quickly blink away because the attending in charge walked up and asked about the patient. I was having a hard time explaining what happened, so I stammered "umm, umm, umm, vomiting..." which he already knew. Eventually, the attending walked away, muttering that he would just go see the patient himself, and I sighed in relief. But I had to get super humble and ask my doctor for suggestions that eventually got me pulled off work and placed in cognitive testing for brain damage, to "more fully evaluate my ability." The testing said I wasn't gravely abnormal, but the main reason I would have trouble is because of the nature of my particular specified, highly academic job.

I returned to work months later armed from my doctors with speech therapy, psychiatric evaluations, and monitoring by what seemed like half the staff in my program. From my church, I was armed with verses, reminders of how great God is, and prayer for complete healing.

But I never got a miraculous healing that fixed all the brain damage. In fact, if I get exhausted now, even years later, I still have word-finding difficulty. I spent the next 1.5 years with symptoms of a concussion, faith that faded into anxiety, and way too many doctors' appointments. Everyone around me prayed for and expected a miraculous recovery—but in that way the answer was *no*. I didn't get a one-time prayer that changed me back to my confident, well spoken, all-memorizing self. But God helped me every single day do a job I shouldn't have been able to do by giving me Holy Spirit power, and I think it's more miraculous that way.

❖ Because I had a Friend who never left my side.

❖ A Helper who would bring something miraculously to my remembrance in spite of my broken brain.

❖ A Strengthener who allowed me to complete every 30-hour shift, even though I was banned from exercise, due to passing out with exertion.

❖ A Provider who incredibly gave me the ability to get through follow-up appointments, and $100,000 hospitalization cost.

❖ A Patient Teacher, who would highlight things I wrote incorrectly, so that we could make the right decisions and treatments for my patients that day.

❖ A Protector, who would direct complicated cases to other teams (people who always get the hardest cases are known in medicine as a "black cloud," but the clouds would always clear up when I was on call).

❖ A Friend and Comforter, who would listen to me cry myself to sleep for months on end, and never wearied of my frustration.

And far too often everything just seemed like a regular, but crazy difficult day. *But when I finished my training three years later, I looked back and saw the miracle that it was for the doctor with brain damage to finish residency with no patients lost, no lawsuits filed, and no wrongful treatments done in spite of myself. I knew it wasn't regular and wasn't because of me. It wasn't exactly what I had prayed for, but it was exactly what I needed—to see the Holy Spirit anoint my job every single day.*

Now, I almost appreciate meningitis because it got me to a place where I wholeheartedly admitted I needed God's help every minute of every day. Honestly, in our careers, it takes a lot of humility to admit God is wiser and ask Him for help. But it's only when you ask expectantly and respond accordingly that God can move.

God doesn't always show up in the way we expect or even the way we ask. But God always hears and responds to our prayers. And if our prayers are for parking spots and for "food to be nourishing to our body" that's totally fine. But couldn't we ask the Creator of the Universe for more? Couldn't we faithfully believe that He show up at our workplace every single day and give us outstanding testimonies? Couldn't we pray ardently for new innovations, new tactics, new ideas, and new life? Couldn't we stop limiting our lives to what we ourselves are capable of doing and instead live them to the full extent of what God raises us up to? What could that look like for you?

Further Questions for Study:

1) Do you feel like you are a blessed/favored person?
   Why or why not?

2) What did you learn about the Holy Spirit in your journey of faith?
   What do you expect from Him in your daily life?

3) What might it look like to allow the Holy Spirit to anoint your daily work?

Church of God

"Then we will no longer be infants, tossed back and forth by the waves, and blown here and there by every wind of teaching and by the cunning and craftiness of people in their deceitful scheming. Instead, speaking the truth in love, we will grow to become in every respect the mature body of him who is the head, that is, Christ. From him the whole body, joined and held together by every supporting ligament, grows and builds itself up in love, as each part does its work."
~Ephesians 4:14-16 (NIV)

"And what more shall I say? For time would fail me to tell of Gideon, Barak, Samson, Jephthah, of David and Samuel and the prophets—who through faith conquered kingdoms, enforced justice, obtained promises, stopped the mouths of lions, quenched the power of fire, escaped the edge of the sword, were made strong out of weakness, became mighty in war, put foreign armies to flight."
~Hebrews 11:32-34

When I was in residency I used to have reoccurring dreams that I was fighting in a literal war. There were multiple fighters against me on the battlefield, but I was the only one fighting back. One time, I was discouraged and kept scanning the field wishing anyone would come help. The scene was always gray and murky, but this time I thought I saw movement in the distance. I squinted my eyes and saw other soldiers a great distance away. They weren't coming to join my fight—they were standing and praying for me. But even more incredible, as I kept scanning the horizon, I saw dozens, and then hundreds, and then thousands of friends lined up on all edges of the field—standing at attention—praying. They weren't fighting the way I wanted, but they were fighting the way I needed—in prayer. Suddenly the battle in front of me seemed less intimidating, as I realized that *I am never truly alone.*

The mission of God to redeem the world using us can be extremely overwhelming if we think about it too hard. If I were severely honest, my life was probably not going to make that big of an impact. Maybe there would be one or two lives at my job that would be changed, but even that would be difficult. And from a redemption standpoint, was I supposed to overhaul the entire health care system myself? This was a truly crazy plan! In the past, no wonder Israel never got it right, and today our churches are pushed to the outer limits of influence—God must have another backup plan!

As I have reflected on who God is—this mission sounds just like Him. The Patient Planner who never does things the way we expect—who spent hundreds of years sending prophets to teach people right versus wrong, and who sent His Son who they killed. But the Father knew they would kill Him, and amazingly enough—that was the plan! And instead of coming with guns blazing and war raging, His son came teaching a simple message of a change of heart. "It's not the revolution we wanted. But it's the one we needed." After setting up this incredible turn of events, He left it up to us—

broken, confused, and distracted, though we may be. He left it up to us to make the choices, and He gave us the ability to turn the tide of culture in more ways than one. Yet far too often we don't use any of the strengths we actually have.

The main strength we have is that God doesn't work in the constraints of our world. He isn't limited by our simple rules, like one plus one equals two. When you get God involved, one plus one equals 5,000. Just think of the miracles of Jesus feeding the multitudes—His power and a boy willing to give his lunch up is all He needed to make things truly multitudinous. Think of Saul's son Jonathan and the young man who carried his armor destroying an army! Where two or more are gathered, God is in their midst— suddenly, it's not just you fighting alone—it's you fighting with an army.

Not everything that you do will be life-changing, but sometimes it's just taking small steps to do your part that speaks mountains to people. And if you jump in and connect with others who are fighting for God's mission—now we've got a success that truly changes things. And that's a battle worth fighting for.

But before you move forward and jump into this fight alone, *find your army.* You need some people to fight with, and some to pray with, but you will need them both in order to go. Where does an army come from? From your church.

I love that Hebrews 10:25 tells us *that we should not give up on the habit of meeting together like so many do,* and I think God's mission is a big part of why. I was studying Church History while writing this book, and I was struck by a number of things. It's amazing how outlandish the church has gone at times. Our entire religion has been thrown so off kilter that it all seems like an evil game of telephone. God says, "love your neighbor," and over 2,000 years, that went from actually loving our neighbor, to ignoring our neighbor, to defaming our neighbor, to literally killing people who do not believe the same things that we do. Craziness!

But what's amazing to me is that even though much has been corrupted over the years, the essential message is still the same. We are still learning from the same Bible with the same truth from the same God who spoke to the disciples and taught us only to love God. That's not some weird accident that God's word has been so preserved. But it's completely, obviously, and amazingly, only thanks to God that we have anything worthwhile left at all.

I read a book written by a physician who was comparing the functioning of the muscles to the functioning (or dysfunctioning) of the church. Our muscles work by contracting—a tense row of linear cells that all shorten tightly, and in doing so, will bend a body part. Muscles can also hold a tensile contraction—staying steady in one position. It's quite interesting, because these two simple movements, either contract or hold, make up all of our movements from walking to dancing a jig. We are able to achieve a million motions, but only if there is a resisting force. You can only bend your arm if you have appropriately relaxed muscles on the opposite side of your arm. If all the muscles in the back and front of your arm simultaneously contracted you wouldn't get anywhere; but if the back can relax and the front contract, you can actually pick something up. Antagonism makes movement possible.

Our churches need to better emulate this. Far too often, some churches end up at odds with others—fighting on opposite sides of the same issue, and allowing it to divide or completely paralyze them. Our call is to be able to bend and stretch. Fight and redeem. Stand up to and bend for. The world needs us to be forgiving and merciful. It needs us to stand against injustice and pain. The way Jesus interacted with people when He was on Earth, wasn't always one or the other—it was *in between the lines* of both.

It's so easy for some Christians to go to the extreme...to the edge of reason with what we know about God, and what we believe He called us to do. In early church history, some leaders believed they were supposed to own nothing and to eat grass; while others were stealing things from the very people they were supposed to serve. *It is the extremes of some Christianity that people don't want to be around*—a crazy religion, surrounded by their own made-up rules, that is either forcing, demeaning, or hating those they were originally meant to serve. We have to know God and His church, the Bride of Christ. We have to be able to keep our footing and stand on the commands in the Bible to sometimes stay and wait, and sometimes fight and bend. We have to learn to live somewhere between what they need and hope for. Somewhere between anger and righteous indignation. Somewhere between complete acceptance of everything and unbending justice as well. It's somewhere *in between* that God has called us to live.

Church history shows us the warring and conquests over the generations—thousands of years of people failing to trust God and seeking their own exaltation above his. Wars where Christianity had to be accepted or you would be beheaded. It's the angry church leaders arguing over inconsequential things that split the church again and again. The inability of people to see the earth and its people the way God sees them. Studying church history is so frustrating because of all the things that have been lost and sacrificed.

But my first teacher in church history taught me that there is always a sliver of people who truly believe, a sliver who trust God no matter how unpopular it is, and a sliver who are willing to go back to the scriptures and back to the foundations of who God is and who He called us to be.

❖ And it's that sliver that laid down their lives in the first few centuries and refused to denounce Christ.

❖ It's that sliver that preached that every person had worth, and fought for women's privileges, and banished the practice of infanticide.

❖ It's that sliver that created hospitals that cared for people.

❖ It's that sliver that tacked their beliefs to a board and insisted that Jesus' grace had saved us, not our own following of the law.

❖ It's that sliver that created universities that furthered our understanding of the world.

❖ It's that sliver that renounced slavery and skin color as a reason for exploiting people.

❖ It's that sliver that gathered in the twentieth century and reminded us of the Holy Spirit as our ever-present help and power.

❖ It's that sliver that will continue to change the face of the earth, even if just as an undercurrent, until Jesus comes back.

❖ And it's that sliver that cannot just sit by idly twiddling their thumbs and waiting, when there's still so much left to fight for!

How can we go from running and avoiding, like the church has done for far too long, to changing the look of a culture? *Start with foundations. We have to go back to the foundations of what God called us to do and see how he is leading us to go from there.* We're not meant to run, not meant to force, not meant to ignore, and not meant to hide. We were called to change the culture, and to change people's lives, not just in the past, but also today.

We also have to stay and believe. We can't ignore the church. We can't do it alone. We can't just "read our Bible" and "listen to online sermons" and consider ourselves set for the rest of our training and work. We have to stay and find your army.

A beautiful thing about the church is that it still manages to look holistically at the problems that normally we would tend to focus on from our own point of view. Faith-based organizations and churches tend to view outreach more holistically. For example, in dealing with the homeless, the government might provide a house; but the church would provide for housing as well as counseling, community outreach, job training, freedom from addictions, and so much more. The church reminds us of the whole picture, whereas our particular field may only see the situation through a single lens. Each person in the church is a different and integral part of the same and whole body.

Although the church is not perfect, it's where we are molded, encouraged, reminded, and directed. And I know—it's hard sometimes...

This church doesn't have others doing the work I do...

This church doesn't do this thing in the community I wanted to help with...

This church isn't jaw-droppingly amazing every service I attend...

You don't know what they said to me...

Believe me, I have personally encountered all of these things—it's not perfect!

God is not calling us to be perfect, He is calling us to walk together.

It's not always the revolution we wanted, but it's the one we needed. We have a vital part to play that must be linked up with others doing their part, in order to complete the mission of God. It doesn't work if you go alone. It works when you link arms with other like-minded saints and go with your army—when you work with others who are just as limited and imperfect as you. Walk with others who sometimes offend, or are mean, or boring, or are imperfectly human. Remember, the church is like a body—only made worthwhile by the gives and takes and the gifts and strengths that all together make it a whole. How are you doing linking arms with those God has called you to walk with?

Further Questions for Study:

1) How are you doing dreaming with others for the things God dreams of?

2) How are you doing staying *in between the lines* of extreme and indifferent?

3) How are you doing being the sliver that stays true no matter what?
   What might that look like in your life?

Changing Our Ministry

Myth of Maturity

"Anyone can disciple others as long as he or she is sincerely endeavoring to follow Christ." ~Steve Murrell

"Write down what you love to do most, and then go do it with unbelievers...
Whatever you love to do, turn it into an outreach."
~Rick Warren

"If Jesus appeared in front of me right now, I would believe in Him!"

"Really? Because I am certain I could talk myself out of believing that happened, and I already believe in Jesus!" I replied incredulously. We laughed at the absurdity, and my two friends agreed with me. We talked for another hour until we realized it was morning and I headed out.

"Thanks so much for talking to us about God and your religion and stuff."

As I got in my car, I realized I had just spent about seven hours talking about "God and my religion and stuff" with two classmates who were agnostic. They still weren't saved, but they learned a lot—and so did I. It was a fun night I will never forget.

53

I didn't go to medical school to witness to or disciple people. I was concentrating on the education I needed so I wouldn't kill people one day! But with good friends, religion is going to come up, so at some point I learned not to run away from those discussions. I wasn't praying for this opportunity with my friends, and had no plan of what to say to their hundreds of questions. But I had learned, *if you just stay and listen, God will give you something to say.*

One of the main things I saw repeatedly in medical school is that the world loves experts. Knowledge in our culture is highly favored—often we value reason above almost anything else. But more knowledge is not always what people need. Sometimes they just need an ear, and amazingly enough, even a low-life med student is good enough for that. I've had patients actually cry when they realized I was leaving—choking out a simple, "But you listen to me!" I could think, "I went to school for eight years and all you care about is that I listen to you?" Or I could appreciate that I don't need another lecture or another degree in order to make a difference in someone's life. I just need to be available.

When the epic string of questions with my friends occurred, I was leaving town the next morning, and I still needed to pack and clean my apartment—but all of that didn't matter as much as just being available for my friends. They will recognize that you took time for them, and your actions really will speak as loudly as your words. Sacrifices don't come at a time that is convenient for you... if they did, they wouldn't be sacrifices.

The second part of what the Lord taught me that night is you don't need all the answers. This is the myth of maturity and Scripture makes this clear time and time again. 1 Corinthians 1:27 tells us that God chose the foolish things of this world to shame the wise and the weak things of this world to shame the strong. He doesn't require that we have any degrees or extra education in order to share His word. All He needs in order to accomplish astonishing things is a heart willing to be used. It's completely backwards from what the world teaches, but oddly enough, admitting that we don't know it all is where we start with God.

In my field, it's often "fake it until you make it." Many doctors would tell you they have no acting skills, but they wouldn't have made it without them! Looking confident and randomly discussing whatever obscure information you do know is how you make it through rounds in med school.

Admitting you don't know it all and asking God to cover your imperfections is how God works in His world. Thankfully, we don't have to be perfect to be used by God, or none of us would ever be useful for anything.

If you've been following God more than a day, you already know more than a non-Christian. I love a story from the book, *Wikichurch*. It describes how a small group in the Philippines started a church that grew to be a megachurch with over 80,000 members. The entire driving force of that growth was discipleship. Discipleship is the process of teaching others how to follow after Christ. The initial group was all brand-new Christians, who led with what little they did know. The leadership preached that all you had to do was stay one book ahead of the person you were discipling, as you were reading through the Bible. It may sound like a faulty plan for those of us who highly value education, but I think the numbers speak for themselves. *You are qualified, right now, today, as is, with all you know so far, to speak to someone else about God.*

On that long, seven-hour series of questions with my friends, I didn't have the answers many times. I was just honest. I shared my testimony, and my own struggles with Christianity. I listened to their negative past experiences with religion, their personal concerns about the validity of the Bible, and fears about the logic of the whole story. Sometimes the Holy Spirit would give me the right response, and other times I had to work through my pride and admit I just didn't know. People don't always need the exact scientific reasoning or historical arguments. They need you to be genuine. If something was unclear I told them I could look it up, or ask a friend, and discuss it with them later.

This experience also reminded me how to keep my eyes open. Discipleship is not a specific plan you need to follow—it's about being available, honest, and friendly. I have friends who can disciple their waitress at a restaurant after a two-minute conversation. I don't have that ability—I'm on the quieter side! But the reason that I saw that happen was that I was really good friends with those two guys—and that in and of itself almost got me into trouble!

Let me just add here—I love to dance. Find me at any wedding and I only stop dancing for brief re-hydration. In college I took dance lessons and participated in shows—but those opportunities were not available in med school. So, I ended up befriending the partiers. I actually sat at their table during our introductory weekend, and then stayed friends with them. They went out regularly to a bar, drank, and danced. And I went with them.

Now to clarify—I did not have an extensive clubbing history—had never done that before, had just turned 21, and it was finally legal. I was always totally sober...I went to dance. I never did anything I wouldn't do in front of my pastor. Before the year had begun, I spent time reading my Bible, and decided in advance where my boundaries were going to be. I wasn't likely to have a problem behaving inappropriately in a club—my weaknesses were not related to that lifestyle. But God gave me the freedom that dancing was going to be alright for me that year—and I'm so glad He did. I made some great friends I wouldn't have had otherwise, and I had a ton of fun.

I also nearly lost some friends. For those of you who read the last paragraph and almost had a heart attack—you might have been on that list. They thought, *"Oh, she's one of those 'Christians' who parties on the weekend and then goes to church on Sunday like she's actually following God."* But I fully believed in God and served Him—even when I was in the club. The more I went, the more I felt confident this was where God wanted me for that year. This is not to say that it's okay for everyone to hang out at the club every weekend. I have a lot of friends that do not drink or go to clubs at all, and I fully honor and respect their decisions. But we do have to take the time and energy to befriend people who are not Christians— sometimes that means going where they are—wherever that may be. I knew these particular friends weren't going to come to church with me. I either had to write them off, or trust that maybe dancing on the weekends was okay for another reason.

Seeds take time to grow. A year later it became a place of ministry. After having made fun of me for my Christianity for months, my friends pulled me aside one night after a concert and asked, "Why are you so different? You have fun in the club but you're never drunk. You are cool and real but say you're a Christian. Tell us about this God you believe in and why."

Later as I reflected on it, I remembered that Jesus went to sinners' homes. He didn't run away from them. He didn't avoid them because they were following different codes of ethics. He loved on everyone, wherever He could.

I love the story of Jesus and Levi in Mark 2. He calls Levi to follow him, reaching out to someone that most Jews would have avoided completely. Tax collectors were the evil politicians and dirty lawyers of the empire—disdained for the work they did. Jesus wasn't worried about reputation, he knew Levi's life was more important than what others thought. He went to Levi's house and ended up eating dinner with all of those evil sinners—and the religious folk went off on Him! *How dare he spend any of his free time doing anything besides teaching in the synagogues?* It's easy to point fingers at people and say they are wrong, but how will "those people" ever know God if the entire church avoids them? Jesus didn't teach by going to the biggest congregation and preaching a moving sermon. He taught by loving on, accepting, and reaching out to the people he encountered every day—often the worst of the worst—the most lost and confused.

Real discipleship is as simple as loving those who God puts in your path.

Sometimes you have to pay attention to discern those God puts in your path.

There is a very long and complicated way that the heart forms when we are in the womb. I think it's quite cool. The heart starts beating about day 21, and at that point it's just a long hollow tube. It takes several weeks for it to basically fold in half, rotate, and close over itself in order to become the incredible four-chambered pumping machine that we have when we are born. The exact way that the heart folds has to be learned in medical school because most of the congenital heart problems that exist are due to improper folding. Suffice it to say, I have simplified the explanation quite a bit, and it's difficult to remember where exactly it can go wrong.

I quite enjoyed this topic. I was told by an upper classman it was going to be a big part of a test, so I read a separate book, and then drew out my own set of diagrams. I mentioned it to several classmates the day before the exam, and then went through teaching them the diagrams as a review. I was not in the crowd of crammers who were going to stay up all night at the school studying, so I picked up my stuff to head home.

But one of my classmates was freaking out. He was visibly upset about all he had left to learn. He was pouring his third cup of coffee and begged me to walk him through the steps I had already taught my other classmates. I apologized and said I was exhausted, but I'm sure he would figure it out, and I left. I honestly didn't think much of it—he was a good student and I was sure he would be fine. I couldn't teach everybody!

The test did have tons of questions about the heart's development. Afterwards, a couple of us were talking and I mentioned I was so glad I had studied the heart so much. The classmate from the night before commented, "If only you had taught me too." He was joking, but I looked in his eyes and felt so convicted. Sometimes discipleship is a mind-bending seven-hour conversation about who God is. But sometimes it's just taking ten minutes out of your busy schedule to lay down your life for someone else. It may be the simplest of things that will speak mountains to someone, if you just take the time.

It's easy to brush people off and blame whatever you like- usually we have legitimate excuses.

But God calls us to love, teach, and serve even when we are exhausted, when we are frustrated, when we are mad, and when we don't know what to say.

Thankfully, when we do step out, even with all our weaknesses, He promises to love on us as we love on other people.

And it's only when God gets involved that something like teaching a classmate or dancing all night becomes something much bigger than it sounds.

As a Christian in the marketplace, you are going to have to make a lot of hard choices in your career. I sat down with

God and my Bible a few months before I started graduate school and wrote out where my goals, my limits, and my boundaries would be. I wrote down my intentions—how often I would go to church, whether or not I would drink, and what I believed about the topics I knew would come up in the classroom. You have to decide where you need to set boundaries for your Christian expectations and for your walk with God. Where you are going to leave people behind and stand for something different. Where you are going to go out of your way and serve someone in patience and love. And where you are going to stand and tell the truth about the faith you have and the God you believe. It won't always end the way you expect. It won't always be as easy as them seeking you out to ask you questions. It won't always be obvious. It won't always be fun. But I guarantee you God will bring you chances to talk to people about your faith and to love on them at work—are you recognizing them and going for it?

Further Questions to Ponder:

1) What boundaries have you set up to help yourself avoid temptations in your life?
   Do any of them keep you from befriending non-Christians?

2) How are you doing recognizing and speaking up in discipleship opportunities?

3) How does the myth of maturity affect you in your career? In your Christian walk?
   Are you confident in who you are and in what God can do?

Just Stop It

"Are you so foolish? Having begun by the Spirit, are you now being perfected by the flesh?"
~Galatians 3:3

A few weeks before starting residency, our bosses gave a talk about how to make it through the grueling work hours. *"Don't think about anything else but work. Hire professionals to clean your house. Put your families on notice that you are not going to be available. Don't spend time thinking about finances, fun, or fitness—pick up those things again after you've finished training. Work hard at the hospital, party hard on your days off, and worry about nothing else."* While I understood what they were saying, it made me cringe inside, but I wasn't sure why.

The workplace demands a lot from us nowadays...to be available at all costs, and to lay down everything else for our jobs. To a certain extent it is required—we have to put in the hours and discipline to properly learn our crafts. However, sometimes more sacrifices are required than are actually needed in order to do our jobs. We have to learn how to find that very thin line that exists between slacking at work and slacking in our daily life.

At the end of residency, I heard a psychologist discussing morality, and I realized what had made me cringe about the recommendations I'd heard years before. He discussed how our lives are like a pendulum. People spend most of their time swinging between one side—control, and the other side—rebellion. Control is when we act appropriately—dutifully giving up our time, doing the right thing, and obeying our superiors. Rebellion is what happens when we get tired of "acting right" and decide to just do our own thing. People live predominantly as a rule-following, well-behaved controller—or as the rebellious, stand out, wild child. When they get tired of behaving one way, they swing all the way back to the other side.

For most of my training, that was exactly how most people were living their lives—rule following and getting everything done during the week, and then crazy partying every weekend to "let off the steam." This is not what God intended. He gave us a set of rules to follow so that we have a clear measurement to judge what is right and wrong.

Those rules were not meant to be followed out of our own self-control, and they were not meant to save us. Jesus worked out all the requirements for our sin, so that our behavior would not determine whether or not we were loved or sanctified. The highly religious will spend their lives hurling back and forth from trying to keep it all together. *The overworked will think it is the only way to survive.* But God didn't have this in mind for us at all.

At this point I should probably give you advice for how to not live life like this—so here is the best I have—*just stop it!*

Stop messing up, stop spinning out, stop worrying about it.

Did that help?

That's often the world's answer for making life better—
"Just stop it!" As a child, I did a science project on quitting
cigarette smoking. People get used to the hand-to-mouth
process of smoking and develop an oral fixation of putting
something into their mouths. Most of the time when people
quit, they replace smoking with something else oral, like
chewing gum—or eating. So, the doctor will say "stop it with
the smoking," and by their next visit they may have gained
thirty pounds. So, next, the doctor says, "stop it with the
overeating." The person may spin out in some other form—
maybe even a healthier one—say physical fitness. They
become obsessed with working out, even to the detriment of
their joints and muscles, and end up with injuries. And what
do you suppose the next recommendation will be?

The root problem wasn't really that the person was
addicted to smoking, or eating, or exercising. Something
deeper is driving the person to obsessive behavior.

Bad Behavior Stems from Bad Thinking

For obsessions and addictions, it's possible the person
is getting a high off the activity they are doing. Or the person
is trying to cover an insecurity they may not even be aware
they have. The first obvious result of sin in the Garden of Eden
was shame. That shame, the result of guilt, caused Adam to
hide himself from God, and break that perfect relationship
with God. God did not condemn them. But their disobedience
created a separation between themselves and God.

65

Additionally, their relationship with other men, work itself, and the Earth was damaged because of the curse of their sin. But Jesus was sent to redeem everything that was lost in the Garden—sin, relationship, illness, curses, everything.

The ultimate issue with obsessions is still listening to the Evil One who accuses of guilt and shame. Just like Adam covering himself with fig leaves, people are still trying to use their own self-control to whip it into shape, and then spinning out of control. They are going to have to face the reality of saying, "Here I am, Lord. I can't do it alone."

Far too often, we use that same approach to use our will and what we can scheme to change people's hearts. That's not discipleship—that's forced willpower.

"I'm having a problem drinking too much alcohol."
Stop it.

"I don't believe that God has the best in mind for me."
Stop it.

"I keep trying to prove myself by my actions."
Stop it!

But you can only stop them for so long before human nature kicks back in. This is crash dieting at its worst—three days of perfect low-calorie vegetables and fruits followed by several hours of too much pizza, soda, and donuts. We can only last so long in our own strength.

I'm a little obsessed with movies, so I've got to give you one more example. I love the *Avengers* first movie. However, the second movie kind of annoyed me. If you don't follow

Marvel, here's the gist of it—the Avengers are a group of superhuman people who have incredible abilities, and the goal is that they come together to fight the battles that humans cannot handle (like crazy space monsters in the first movie). So, the Hulk has incredible brute strength, Iron Man his awesome suit, Thor his big hammer, and Captain America his guidance. In the second movie, there is a computer program that gets compromised, takes on an evil personality, and wants to destroy the world. He uploads himself to the Internet and is doing major damage. So, they go after him—fighting this hard drive, destroying that mainframe! During the movie I got so exasperated, trying desperately to send brain waves through the screen to the characters to get a new battle plan. Let's be real—you can't kill the Internet with a gun or a really good punch—no matter how strong you are! You could destroy a computer. You could kill a person. You could delete a file, but unless you get back to the source of the problem or the millions of connections that can get on wi-fi, you just plain can't kill the Internet with a gun!

But it's exactly what we do in our lives so often. We go after our sin, after other's problems, after our negative thoughts with the only weapon we know—we assume our own actions and self-control can shoot down the very thing that's destroying our life. We cannot live our lives the way the world does, spinning our wheels on our own hard work. And for those of us who are able to keep the negative actions at bay for a while—it leaves us with a whole lot of pride in our own abilities and looking down at those around us who don't have as much self-control. As the Bible puts it, "Having begun by the Spirit, are you now being perfected by the flesh?

(Galatians 3:3)." I don't know about you, but I used to do it all the time.

I started college as a bad perfectionist—I wanted good grades. When I admitted that how God saw me was more important than my own life plans—I set out to change my faulty habits. *Just stop it.* But as soon as I tried, I got confused. I *wanted* to "just stop it," but I couldn't stop the perfectionist behavior entirely—I would've failed college! I still needed to study, but how much was reasonable? Was 16-hours-a-day inappropriate, and 2-hours-a-day better? Was two hours of studying a good choice since I was taking six classes? If I didn't get good grades, was that now a good thing? If my problem wasn't an activity you could totally stop, how could I even know where the line was between right and wrong?

If you haven't picked up on the trend, here it goes again... The answer is somewhere *in between the lines.*

**Because it's *in between the lines* of having your actions determine your value,
and knowing that your actions still have value
that we need to live in the marketplace.**

We want to create things that are excellent, because our excellence glorifies God. The things we create are echoes back to the amazingness of our God, the Creator of the universe, who gave us the ability to walk in His footsteps. When He calls us to a certain profession, He doesn't call us there to watch us fail, but to help us redeem and create and sow, where darkness has reigned for far too long.

As I started giving up my identity to God, slowly but surely my desire to prove myself by my grades dropped. Even my hours spent studying dropped. I was still premed and still spent a lot of time studying (so many long Saturday nights), but it wasn't because of an insatiable desire to *impress*—it was a desire for *excellence*. And my grades—amazingly stayed the same! When you give your work to God first, He protects that which matters the most.

I started my sophomore year off as a happier, less-mean, less-overworked person. I took over as choreographer of a fun Filipino dance called Modern Tinikling. It was my first year choreographing, and though I was neither a professional nor even Filipino, I wanted it to be legit. I spent hours watching similar performances, listening to songs, and writing out pages of group formations. *Somewhere along the way it went from being "let's do a good dance" to "let's be better than anyone else ever has!"* Later, when I started to have dreams about dance steps, I realized something was wrong. It was perfectionism and moralism, right there again—destroying yet another part of my life! I just needed to stop my negative thoughts about myself and move on. *Just stop it.*

I got more involved in campus ministry and took over as worship director. I recruited musicians, taught songs, and sang myself as well. It started out well. But eventually, I started to realize that I was getting testy when people would change plans last minute. I was spending hours doing things that weren't my responsibility. I was more worried about how many people were at the practice than whether or not we were actually worshiping God. *I finally admitted that perfectionism had found me yet again, even at church!* I thought I was free from this sin and had given it to God—but it just kept showing up again and again! *Just stop it.*

I was frustrated and about to give up trying, but instead was lovingly taught that this was all normal—that we become increasingly aware of our own imperfections as we continue to live our lives. That what we know about ourselves on day one when we meet Jesus, is very different than what we know on day 500—because God continually works to reveal more parts of our lives that are not totally under His control.

The goal isn't that we pretend that these new struggles don't exist. The goal isn't that we work harder to stamp them out of our life for good. The goal isn't even that we admit that we are broken and give up entirely.

The goal is the cross.

It is common for Christians to think of the cross on day one of salvation and then to move on from there. To learn new things about Christianity, about God, about everything that makes us "more mature Christians." But the goal isn't that we "move on." All we have to do is understand the cross more deeply. As we get to know God, we become increasingly aware of our own limitations and God's perfection. It is actually quite disheartening, so we don't usually want to dwell there. Some Christians may live in deception, refusing to admit that they are trying to fill up the broken spots with their own excuses, or their hard work, like I did.

Well, I may still be a perfectionist, but I'm using it for the church—that must make it okay, right?... My future patients need me to be a perfectionist—doesn't that make me a better doctor?

I could continue to live in deception, making excuses for my behavior. Or I could admit that I was still very imperfect, marvel at the greatness of God, so unlimited compared to me, and I could thank Him that He sent Jesus to save the completely crazy, totally overworked, nuthouse perfectionist of me. I could go back to what happened at the cross and admit that I don't really see myself as special. Admit that I feel like a lineup of many, many people that God died for. I just want to be loved and appreciated for me, and if I work hard enough, I feel important. Admit that it is all a misunderstanding in my understanding of my loving Father God; and ask Him to heal my heart, and help me to accept the worth, the value, and the love He has already given me that I had been trying to get from my accomplishments.

It's not my actions at all that determine my worthiness to be loved and accepted. It goes back to understanding all that the blood of Jesus on the cross covered, and how the willing sacrifice of His life changed all of eternity. What an incomparable thing He did in a single action.

And it's changing our thinking that makes the cross and what Christ did more and more important in our lives every day—so that the rest of the things in our lives, however disheartening, become less and less important. It makes us stop struggling with the exact same problem again and again. And we start to look more like Christ as we let go of things that probably just plain don't matter that much anyway.

I put this important lesson under the heading of discipleship because here's the warning: *I can see your behaviors, I cannot see your heart.* For those discipling or teaching me over the last few years through my perfectionism—I still studied, I still worried about tests, I still got nervous about evaluations and I still questioned my worth for years.

You can't always look at someone's behaviors and determine exactly how much their heart is changing.

Sometimes we can see noticeable changes in people's lives; but only God knows if they are truly getting closer to Him. Eventually, God changes our thinking, and our external behaviors really do change. But it's easy for us to want to skip the "God step" and get to the "noticeable changes" part. Knowing that only God can transform us, and that it usually takes longer than we expect—we have to be patient in discipleship, and concentrate not on actions, but on God—no matter what.

What does this have to do with work? Whatever you do to yourself, you will do to others as well. This is one reason why some Christians run around avoiding those "evil sinners"—they're focused more on a person's behavior than on God. If we stop looking at good behaviors to give people worth, we will be less judgmental with the people God has placed in our lives. It makes a huge difference when we start to disciple people, because it changes how we interact with them. It's easy to tell someone else to stop their negative behavior. It's an entirely different thing to help them see how much God loves them in spite of their sin, died for them without giving it a second thought, redeemed their lives, and anointed them with the power to walk away from it. Obviously, that's a much more time-consuming process. But when you get there, people notice because it's real. And that's the kind of change that truly lasts.

Further Questions for Study:

1) Do you have examples of things in your life where you try to "just stop it," instead of going to the source of the problem?

2) How do you get to the source of a problem in your life, and let God change your heart first, and your actions later? What would it look like to apply the cross to your biggest problem right now?

3) How do you make boundaries for how much work is reasonable and healthy for you? How can you draw your line between excellence and crazy?

True Success

"What we sacrifice for the most is the object of our worship."
~Chip Ingram

"Keep your heart with all vigilance, for from it flow the
springs of life."
~Proverbs 4:23

"I have learned that success is to be measured not so much by the
position that one has reached in life as by the obstacles which he
has overcome while trying to succeed."
~Booker T. Washington

I'm told I was quite mean when I started college. It's a funny thing to say, because now people usually say I'm sweeter than candy. But at the start of college I was just plain mean. Personally, I think the more accurate description would have been "ultra-focused," but perhaps I am being easy on myself. But here's how it played out—you tried to get too close to me, and I just kind of blocked you out. It wasn't on purpose. It wasn't even a conscious decision. But it was there. I was terrified of letting anybody in to see what I saw deep down inside myself—a monstrous and insecure mess.

I had given my life back to God, understood and truly lived lordship, and had gotten baptized in the Holy Spirit. But one thing that I remember vividly was the very last day of freshman year. It's the best example of discipleship I've ever known. Naima was a senior in the campus group and planning

74

to become a campus minister. She was a straight-laced African American girl with a big heart and a quick tongue, and spent the year discipling me. Basically, that meant she was chasing me, dodging my mean comments, and sometimes succeeding in getting me to do Bible study with her. I wasn't exactly a willing candidate, but I was glad she was diligent. And I didn't realize how hard she worked until the last day of school.

I went to college when people still had dorm phones with answering machines. (Cell phones really came into use my second year.) I was cleaning out my room when I realized the answering machine had 28 saved phone messages that needed deleting. I expected them all to be my mom or my best friend—who else did I ever talk to? I pressed play and sat back to listen...in complete silence I realized all the messages were from Naima. All 28. Most of them were a simple, "Ashley, where are you? We should hang out." As much as I had appreciated the Bible verses and church meetings, I had just wanted to feel that God loved me. As I listened to her calling me repeatedly, even though I had been ignoring her, I broke down. She had modeled how much God pursues us—whether we want Him around or not!

More than anything, it showed me that discipleship is just determined friendship.

One thing that I do now because of Naima is look around for the meanies. I was hurting and terrified to admit it, so I just covered it up and kept everyone else out. Your coworkers, classmates, and family that are difficult to even be around may have been placed there just so you could love on them, in spite of their rough edges. Your caring doesn't have to be anything miraculous—maybe just leaving a few messages showing that you care.

When I was a kid, I loved polishing rocks. Some of my favorites were the agates. They're the ones that look like boring, greyish-brown lumps on the outside, but when broken open are filled with layers of gorgeous gem colors. Rock tumbling is the process of polishing stones so they look pretty all over—you put them in a barrel and let them tumble for hours. Agates are often formed by volcanic explosions, under extreme pressure, which creates thick layers. If you tumble them too fast, they simply crack—you have to tumble them slowly and handle them with care. They are often overlooked because they blend in with the surroundings, but once buffed to round their rough edges, they reveal their hidden jewels. Discipleship is like that—slowly knocking off the hard bits in people's lives, until the remarkable person they are inside is uncovered.

I spent years being friends with a "rough-edged" person at church, frequently defending their off-putting behaviors to my other friends. But I had literally befriended them because I saw them as a stone that just needed some polishing.

But the only reason I knew how to do that is because someone had done it for me.

Discipleship is the process of helping someone become more like Christ. It's a lifelong process, one that we will always be slowly "tumbled" into. I'm suspecting that in your chosen field you are going to run across several of these people. I've had a boss who called me *useless* and *replaceable.* I've had fellow students who took credit for my ideas and bad-mouthed me in front of our teachers. I've worked around grouchy, mean-spirited people who never woke up on the right side of the bed—for years! And I am sure that you will too. You cannot repay evil for evil. God will place in your life some who are very much like you, and easy to love. And He will place those in your life who are crazy, spiteful, and competitive—ones you just want to get away from—*but who are also made in God's image.* They still need your respect, your patience, and your love—even if you never get any back.

Jesus tells us in Matthew 28:19-20, to "go and make disciples of all nations, baptizing them in the name of the Father and of the Son and of the Holy Spirit, and teaching them to observe all that I have commanded you. And behold, I am with you always, to the end of the age." Known as the Great Commission, these words instruct us not to "convert people" or "assume they will learn by our example," but for us to purposefully teach them.

The disciples were sent into a world that didn't know anything about Jesus. They could not simply walk up to a nonbeliever anywhere, give a moving sermon, pray a prayer with them, and then go to the next town. They were coming up against polytheism, varied world views, and people who didn't care at all about religion—actually very similar to the world we live in. But for anyone God put in their path, the disciples would do their best to love them, pray with them, and demonstrate to them how to truly walk with God. New Christians are basically like babies that have to be fed and trained, or else they won't make it far in their relationships with Christ.

The goal of discipleship is to become like Jesus...to have the mind of Christ, and to walk as He walked. And why is this a worthy goal to pursue? We are referred to as Christians in the Bible three times, but called disciples 284 times. It's kind of a big deal. We can all name people in our lives who said they were Christians, but acted in ungodly ways—making us question whether Christianity was real. The ultimate goal is to become more Christ-like so when people look at you they see Jesus—not your perfect exterior, or resumes, or accomplishments. Just Him. Are you valuing discipleship as much as God does?

True and Lasting Success

The world has very specific definitions of success— money, clout, fame, reputation, and job titles go a long way in our fields. But God has a much bigger goal than just what is on our to-do list for today. Think through what you currently have in your head as success. A good way to do it is to write down what you would like your life to look like in ten years. Grab a piece of paper, and jot some things down. Write down what you would be doing, who would be in your life, what your environment would look like, and what your new goals would be at that time. If everything went perfectly, what would success look like for you? What things do you notice that you spend a lot of time thinking about or working on now? What else is hard for you to write, but you are still hoping will become a part of your life one day?

Got it? Did you actually write anything down? I've read many books where it told me to answer some questions and write something down and I just ignored it. I still really encourage you to do it, even if you are one of those people too! When you are finished, read through the story below, and we'll come back to our dreams in a bit.

I watched an incredible movie a few months ago called "Something the Lord Made." It's based on a true story about two men that researched and created the surgery that now saves thousands of children's lives every year. There are a lot of things that can go wrong with a baby's heart as it is formed. Any holes actually lead to the child not being oxygenated well, because blood flow is misdirected—causing what's known as blue baby syndrome. It is very difficult to perform surgery on a beating heart, so it was initially thought that all of these children would die, and that was the only way it could be.

In the 1930s and 1940s, Dr. Blalock and his assistant Vivien Thomas started working on a way to bypass the heart—to move blood flow in a different way around the heart so that the babies could live longer. The movie is a great story about medical advances and racial tensions, as Thomas is actually a black man who has not gone to medical school at all, but he learns how to perfect the procedure on animals. Blalock actually compliments Thomas' skills at surgery by saying his stitches are so perfect they are like "something the Lord made." They work on this procedure for years, finally trying it on the first child on November 29, 1944. But it wasn't until we got that far in the movie that I realized what the ending was going to be.

The surgical procedure that we learn as medical students is called a BT shunt—short for a Blalock-Taussig shunt. Dr. Taussig was the person caring for the little girl who had the first surgery done. Have you noticed the problem yet? Vivien Thomas is not included in the title at all. It's not called a BTT shunt! The man who worked for decades to perfect the surgery and develop the procedure is not even recognized. Dr. Blalock and Dr. Taussig became world renown and helped thousands of children survive. Vivien Thomas lived barely above the poverty line, was never able to go to medical school and be given the title doctor, although he performed thousands of surgeries, and many times was discriminated against in his own hospital. Vivien Thomas did not get any recognition for being a part of creating the shunt until 1985— forty years later. Now put yourself in Vivien's shoes and tell me—would it have been worth it? Was he successful? Would you have kept working there if that was you?

One way God has to work on our hearts in the marketplace is to change our definition of success. Take a look back at the list you wrote down. What are you valuing most as success? Money? Recognition? Accreditation? Creativity? Vacation time? Family? Innovation? Relationships? Now to be real—did you write down that you hoped to disciple and evangelize people in your place of work or study? Did you write down that you hoped God would use your skills and give them Holy Spirit power to create something new in your field that has never been seen before? Did you write down character issues that you prayed God would eliminate by then? Are you dreaming in your own strength, or in the places of impossibility that God can take you? Nothing that you wrote down is evil or wrong—but *are you dreaming for success in your eyes, or success in God's eyes?*

When I finished residency and started looking for jobs I got pretty frustrated because of my personal lack of success. I was ready to quit medicine because of all the personal frustrations and patient problems I had seen. I had struggled with a long bout of physical brain damage that left me with very low confidence, and little professional gain. I had a few teachers who wrote me good recommendations, but most saw me as average. Much of my free time had been spent at my own doctor appointments; and I had no new professional work, academic research published, and no new activities in the medical field. I had my degree, but in the U.S., that was not very impressive, compared to other prospective applicants. It was a crushing blow to my ego, as I realized I had almost nothing you would call success in my field or in the life that I had dedicated 11 plus years to. I was not successful at all according to the world.

I could sit there and complain about that—blame my illness, time spent volunteering at church, or the hours spent talking to friends about God. It's easy to place blame, get angry, or give up when things don't go as expected. But I wrote this chapter of the book to remind myself that blame gets me nowhere, and I simply needed to admit that success in God's eyes doesn't always look like a perfect life in the world's eyes. We usually define success as particular results, but God does not. *Success in God's eyes looks like a heart longing to serve Him every day. It looks like a faith that trusts Him no matter what is crumbling around you. It looks like a life desiring to glorify Him, even if it doesn't glorify ourselves.*

Success to God is faithful obedience, not perfect completion.

❖ True success for God was taking a murderer with a speech impediment, and making him the leader of a million Israelites, as they wandered the desert for forty years — Moses.

❖ True success for God was a seventy-year-old woman laughing in His face as He promised her a son—and then having her wait another thirty years to see that impossible promise come true — Sarah.

❖ True success for God was a king amassing a fortune and drawing plans for an incredible church that he was never allowed to build — David.

❖ True success for God was a righteous man having all his earthly possessions and health taken away, because the devil wanted to test him — Job.

❖ True success for God was sending his own Son, who the entire country thought was going to save them from Roman rule, and letting him die a heinous death on a cross — Jesus.

True success for God doesn't always look like true success to man. Sometimes it honestly just looks like defeat. But great is your reward for refusing to give in. It's usually when you give up the things that have become your idols—things that you hold more important than God—that God can truly move.

In most of the stories above I stopped in the middle— where it gets the hardest and seems the most impossible! Where you exist *in between the lines* of what you hoped and worked for, and wonder if that's all you're going to get. Where you know the vision—and are ready for the payout of the time and energy you put in. The eventual earthly reward for that payout will only last a few seconds before it fades. But the reward for a life dedicated first to God, and secondly to our own success, is an eternal one that cannot be measured in gold. Are you willing to trust Him no matter what that success looks like for you?

So how do we rewrite our goals for success? It begins with getting to know God well. Knowing His impeccable character shows us we can trust Him more than we can trust our advisers and our own goals. He's got our best interests at heart and nothing is impossible for Him.

Often, God takes His dreams for our lives and writes them deep on our hearts so they feel like ours. He gives us big dreams that require His help, and sometimes require momentary sacrifices. He asks us to relax our grip on things we have held too tightly. But then He shows up to bless and amaze, with what we couldn't have conceived on our own. The key to true success is that it always involves Him. It involves dreams bigger than you can do on your own, because He is the completer of the work He gives us to do.

God sees the whole picture and the end results as well as knows how our success impacts our friends and family. I don't think we dream enough about how much God loves the people at our work or school, and wants them to know His love too. We don't dream about ways to strike up a lunchtime conversation, to encourage the person next to us, even ways to initiate changes in the way we do our job. We think our presence will be enough. We hope that they can discern that we are a Christian, see we live a nice life, and receive a smile from us. That is called fear—not discipleship.

"Are We Nice or Are We New?" is another great sermon I heard a few years ago. The pastor questioned whether the goal of Christianity was to be nice to people or to tell them about Jesus Christ. Fear can change us into something we are not. Was the point of the gospel—Jesus dying on a cross for us—just a *get out of jail free* card, or was it meant to change us? Every minute of every day we have the opportunity to advance God's kingdom—are we taking that opportunity? Are we letting fear convince us to stay quiet or stand in faith?

I have known a lot of people who think "their example" will get people saved. Rarely someone may be saved by Jesus miraculously appearing to them in a dream. But far more often, someone in their life has been willing to start a hard conversation about what they believe and why.

A favorite pastor of mine, Pastor Gregg Tipton puts it like this,

**"If you're not telling people about what Jesus did in your life,
He probably hasn't done much."**

You've got a story to tell and a love to give—incredible things God has done in your life. God created the entire universe with just words—what could he create with your story? Are you willing to share? Will you treat sharing that experience as valuable and as great as graduation, vacation, marriage, publishing, tenure, or whatever else success currently means to you?

Further Questions for Study:

1) How are you doing looking for the "ultra-focused" people in your life?
   How are you doing loving on them in spite of their edges?
   What are simple ways to improve on that?

2) Has your definition of "success" changed over the last 5-10 years as you've pursued your goals?
   Where do you think these definitions come from?

3) What does it take to dream like God instead of dreaming like the world does?
   How do you think He would see and work for success in your current position?

4) Why do you think Vivien Thomas stayed and worked in a place for 40 years without acknowledgment/accreditation/advancement?
   Would you if God asked you to?
   Why or why not?

Releasing Kings

"If you are a Christian you are in ministry."
~Joyce Meyer

"If you believe everybody is going to criticize you,
you'll behave cautiously.
If you believe you're probably going to fail,
you're going to venture out tentatively.
If however, you believe that the one true Lord God is
calling you, empowering you, leading you, equipping you,
then you will live boldly. Why?
Because boldness is behavior born of belief."
~Craig Groeschel

We go to church. We go to one more conference, one more worship night, read one more Bible study and wait for it to change us. But the only way we really learn how to minister is to go and do. We have the ability and the responsibility to reach out to those around us and to tell them about God.

Well, Ashley, I invited so and so to church and they said no—what else do you want from me?

Here's a crazy thought—maybe you could personally share the gospel with them.

But that's not my job! My job is restaurant inspector #4 and that's what I do—the pastor is the one who leads people to Christ!

You're right, *sometimes* the pastor leads people to Christ, that's what we expect—but, that is not how the Bible lays it out. Let's go back to the Old Testament and look at how things were described.

Releasing Kings is a book that compares those called to the workplace with those called to ministry. In the Old Testament, the pastors were known as priests. They were a specific group appointed by God. In the New Testament, they would guide people who were getting to know Christ, and were building the church. They counseled, shepherded, healed, married, and buried. The main thing that is confused far too often—they were not appointed to evangelize. That was the job of the kings.

The *kings* are described as those who work in the marketplace. The *kings* were those meant to make society run—the teachers, the shopkeepers, the leaders, and the builders. Largely, these are the names we remember—Shepherd David, Doctor Luke, King Solomon, Soldier Gideon, etc. Many of the important people in the Bible were not actually working in the church, but working as an extension of it. Their jobs were to do their daily physical work, and it was also to lead those around them. Biblically, kings were a crucial part of the church, because they were the ones who interacted every day with non-believers. Their job was to bring the non-believers to faith, and to encourage them in their faith. The goal then, is for those in the ministry (the priests), to push and encounter us (the kings) to go into the world as the hands of God, to *go* and *lead* and *serve*.

The concept is a great example of how kings and priests work together, but most people are not just one or the other—even in the Bible, Jesus worked many years as a carpenter, before going into full-time ministry. The concept is simply a way we should think of interacting with those around us. Our pastor rarely gets to interact with the people who we study and work and serve with every day. It is not our pastor's job to share the good news with them. It is ours.

The most heartbreaking books in the Bible to me are the history books—Kings and Chronicles. You can summarize everything the books say in a single statement: *When the kings did whatever they wanted, so did their followers; but when the kings followed God, everyone did.* Kings are the leaders of society, and their influence affects the faith of everyone around them. You are not a literal king or president, but as a person in the workforce, you have a level of influence. We influence our family and the things they believe. We influence coworkers and the things they live out. We influence not only those below us on the ladder, but also those above us—especially when they see how we take a stand to do things differently than the rest of the world. We are noticed because of our actions, our beliefs, and our principals. We can look like the rest of the world, or accept that we have the ability to influence others every single day.

The most incredible example I have of being noticed by the world is during my bout with meningitis. I used to drive-through and get Krispy Kreme donuts every other week or so.

After being in the hospital, it was several weeks before I had an appetite for them. The drive through attendant had missed me and was worried about me! Who is it in your life that you don't "lead" but actually have an impact on?

Who is aware of the habits you keep, the decisions you make, and the person you are, even when you think no one is looking?

Being a king comes with perks. Kings get the job done. The priest Ezra spent 100 years trying to rebuild a wall around Jerusalem. Nehemiah did it in 52 days. Kings are good at focusing on the goal and making sure it is completed. They take people with them, ministering to them as they complete their goals. Kings are blessed to prosper, because God blesses their natural gifts. Just like with Bezalel, the Bible gives multiple examples of God's anointing on kings' very labor— anointed to create, engage in battle, and lead. Truly blessed kings in the Bible remembered first and foremost who God is and emulated Him. We were created in God's image and have the ability to create, to conceive, to dream, and to accomplish in the same way He does.

Another important idea *Releasing Kings* pointed out was, that *being in the marketplace is not a lesser calling*. Not everyone thinks of it like that, but it seems to be an underlying secret dread that many have. God "called and anointed the pastors," but we just picked a job? Doesn't that make it less special? Where does that idea come from? Why the disconnect between the workplace and the church? Between the pastor and the CEO? I blame much of it on dualism. This is a Platonian concept, conceived thousands of years ago and yet still very pervasive within much of our culture today, although not usually expressed in those terms.

Plato taught that the material world was not as good as, or was more evil than, the spiritual world. He made the goal for people to escape their bodies and their natural instincts, and get to spiritual "betterness" or perfection. This idea re-emerged right after the establishment of the church with the idea of gnosticism. The goal at the time was for people to downplay their natural selves as much as possible, and spend their time in "higher," spiritual pursuits such as prayer, fasting, or spiritual meditation. This same idea permeates our lives even today. Spending time in church or praying, is "better than" working in construction or having a regular job, right? Giving is "more important than" making money, right? Fasting is "more holy than" eating a Thanksgiving meal, right? It's often an unspoken belief, but it is there. But that is not what the Bible shows at all. God created the world, the trees, the animals, the earth and said, "it is good." He didn't create Eden and say "that's satisfactory, but hopefully they'll get to a church service soon!" He placed man there to "work and take care of the earth and fill it with His glory." So, the goal should not be avoiding the "regular, worldly things," it should be entering the world and redeeming what was broken in the fall. Our goal should not be to hate the world and the lives we live, but to take something that God already declared good, and to use our gifts to make them great.

Well, Ashley, that's all fine and dandy, but these are really old concepts—the Old Testament traditions and Plato don't affect our lives that much—and Jesus made all things new when He came in the New Testament.

Totally right! And here was the new plan, "Go into all the world and proclaim the gospel to the whole creation..." *(Mark 16:15).*

This was the plan given to the fisherman, and doctors, and tax-collectors, and to *all* followers of Christ. Not just to the church. Not just to the rabbis. Not just to the priests. It was given to everyone. So, whereas our full-time jobs may not be in full-time ministry, it is a command that Jesus gave, that we should all look for opportunities to tell the world about Christ.

I heard the silent groans from those of you who said that evangelism is not allowed at work. Just look at the evening news—story after story of Christians being fired, or losing a court case, or having trouble at work because they stood up for their faith, or tried to tell someone about Christ. I understand that concern, and we do need to act in wisdom—but not in fear. When I was in medical school I chose to work on a research project with a doctor I knew from church. My advisor at the school recognized the name and told me to consider getting another mentor. I was really surprised at his concern and asked why. He replied something like, "She's a Christian and she's always preaching at people. Both she and her husband are always talking about God. You can work with her if you want to, but I don't recommend it." When further questioned about if there were any concerns with leading capabilities, or work created, he admitted that she would be excellent as a mentor. It occurred to me that I was afraid of sharing my faith at school sometimes, but my mentors, who were obviously doing it quite a bit, were never fired, reprimanded, or punished for it. I was more afraid than I needed to be.

Jesus actually promised us persecution as Christians. Sometimes that's from a friend or family member, and sometimes it will come at work. I have personally never been written up for God. But when it's all said and done, I view my life as working for God, not for that company.

I trust my Boss will take care of me even when the company does not.
I'd much rather live in that honesty and trust than fear and worry.

Now for those who don't do evangelism regularly, it can seem like a big deal. But I promise you, it's going to be fine.

During the last year of my residency, I went on a medical mission trip with a group called *Ten Days* to India. I taught at the college about handling stress for one day. We spent a day doing check-ups on children ministered to by the local the church. We spent a day teaching worship. But the rest of the time, the goal was to evangelize. We were to meet one-on-one with the people we had met throughout the week and to tell them the gospel. We had this nifty little thing called "The God Test," that is, ten quick questions to ask people about their faith, and then share about yours. It seemed really easy. Yet I was terrified, because for all my supposed knowledge and my Bible studies, it had been many, many years (like eighteen years) since anyone had actually given their life to Christ under my direction. I was terrified this whole ability to evangelize had totally passed me up. Also, we were in India, a land of many gods, and we were told it was not common to have people get saved quickly. But I had been praying for it since I signed up for the trip, and hoping God would just overlook my poor evangelizing history.

Throughout the week I became really good friends with a young college student named Harpeet. She was actually from another country and clearly missed home. She angrily complained about how little the other students cared to learn about her awesome heritage. I realized she needed more than just someone to listen to her—she needed a friend in God. So, we had time to talk about Him, but then I chickened out and didn't say anything. Amazingly enough, she came to church on our very last day of the trip. The pastor gave a great sermon on Jesus as our Savior, and I turned to her, ready to agree with her as she got saved. But she didn't, and church was over. I knew this was my last chance to preach the gospel. So, hands literally shaking I reached down fumbling in my purse for like an hour looking for the God Test. I pulled it out and started asking her the wrong questions that you would ask to someone who is an atheist. I skipped an entire page, got completely confused when she explained her beliefs, and figured we were done. But the last question asks you to share about the gospel. So, I gave a long-winded, probably very confusing summation of the sermon, leaving out some important parts that she probably needed to know and just waited, nerves on edge for her to reject it. But instead she said she wanted to know Jesus for herself, and I led her in a shaky prayer to accept Him as her Savior. And a few hours later, I got on a plane and headed back home.

The more I reflected on the whole thing, I figured that it didn't really happen. I prayed for her, frequently asking for

God to forgive the mess that was that encounter. I prayed that God would speak to her in another way.

A few years later, I got involved helping plan medical missions trips *(can we say ironic, given my fear of having to leave school and become a missionary so many years before!).* We planned a trip back to Mumbai. I was looking forward to seeing some familiar faces and getting to follow-up with my friend Harpreet, praying I hadn't totally screwed up her life.

How incredibly surprised I was to find that she was one of the student ministry leaders on campus, totally on fire for God, praying about where God was leading her next. Thankfully, in spite of my awkward inability to convey what Jesus did, God still spoke to her. For someone who doesn't get to lead someone to Christ every day, that's a very reassuring thing to remember.

Getting Ready to Share Our Faith

In medicine, there is well-known phrase passed down by teachers to learn procedures called *"see one, do one, teach one."* You spend the majority of the first two years in the classroom, learning book knowledge. When you first start doing procedures, you are filled with theoretical book knowledge, but very little practical knowledge. As an example, I was walking one day as a medical student, carrying my books, my stethoscope, my papers in my starched white coat pocket, and going confidently through the hospital when someone stopped me.

"Excuse me, ma'am, do you know where the nearest bathroom is?"

I just stood there stammering "uhh, uhh..."

For all my supposed knowledge and time spent studying—I had literally no clue where the nearest bathroom was! Eventually the poor guy just wandered away to find someone else who actually had valuable information. This is the gist of being a student. I think most graduate schools make you feel like "the pus that infects the mucus that cruds up the fungus that feeds on the pond scum..." you can try really hard and still not help at all!

You feel the same as you start trying to learn procedures. For instance, intubating is placing a tube into a person's airway so that you can assist them with breathing. You can watch a hundred videos of intubating on the internet. You can read multiple articles, and know all the right terms and necessary equipment. But—the only way to learn the procedure—is to do it.

"See one, do one, teach one." You start with *"see one,"* meaning you watch as a trained professional does the procedure. But then, the hardest part, you *"do one."* The temptation is to say, "let me just watch one more" or "let me practice on the dummy once more..." but the problem is, there is no *"in between the lines"* here, between getting all the knowledge and using it. You just have to try it. And once you've tried it, the next step in the phrasing is *"teach one,"* meaning you teach how the procedure should go, to someone else who doesn't know how. It solidifies all the things you learned.

It is the same with our faith. We can read book after book, attend conference after conference, podcast all the good sermons, and go to all the right meetings about sharing our faith. But the only way to actually learn it, is to just do it! As we do it and teach it, we start to see things come together more clearly. We won't always know all the answers, or necessarily pull it off perfectly the first time, but the only way to learn is— *to just go!*

Lastly, we have to go in the right mindset. I had a good friend in college who used to help me choreograph our dances. He was not a Christian and really didn't have an interest in faith at all. One day I got to talk with him about why. He said he had been invited to a Christian camping retreat once when he was in high school. They were hiking, eating a lot, and having a great time. That night while everyone was at the campfire, the friend who had invited him pulled him aside and preached the gospel to him. My friend was not interested in accepting Christ as his Savior and turned him down. They talked for a while more, the Christian getting upset and flustered, so he went and got another person from the retreat. That person also tried to convert my friend. Then another. Then another. Then another. When my friend told me this story I was appalled and I apologized on behalf of Christians, and on behalf of God for that long, inappropriate night. God is love.

Trying to force someone to follow what you believe is not love.

God loves us, and in His love gives us the choice, the decision to follow Him or not. It's not a decision to follow a loving God if it is forced—that's just fear. "When we communicate to the world about the God they have yet to meet, it is essential that we communicate light, life, and love."

God loves the person we are talking to. He loved them so much He died for them. He would do anything for them. We cannot approach non-Christians in any spirit other than that love. If we approach them as a notch on our belt of conversions that must comply, we will not be sincere. If we approach them as a requirement for our own salvation, we will not be in the right. If we force them to make decisions they are not sure about, their faith will not last. Evangelism is a mandate given to us, but if we are not going from God's heart, we need to pray that He change our perceptions before we speak and hurt people badly. It's *in between the lines* of pushing people a little, and forcing them a lot, that God moves. Thankfully, it's *in between the lines* of our imperfections, in spite of our fears, and in the midst of very unlikely stories that God really moves and changes lives. Trust Him to do so through you.

I have had many conversations with friends, classmates, and coworkers over the years about God. Many of these people have not gotten saved. Not everyone that we talk to will get saved. We can blame mistakes, misspoken words, and other factors. But I've heard it said that most people need seven steps of contact before they actually commit to following God. Meaning they need to have conversations or experiences with God seven times before deciding to follow Him fully. I am totally confident and comfortable being number one, or two, or six... and not having the testimony of being number seven. This book is about all the gray areas of life that are not how you expected them to be—even when it comes to someone's salvation. Sometimes we're just a part, and the *testimony* doesn't come until years later, and that's okay.

There's a great story about the famous George Mueller. He was believing God for five friends, and spent many years praying for them to be saved. Only one of his friends was saved before he died. The others were not saved until years after his death, two of whom gave their lives to God at his funeral. He never saw the outcome of his prayers, but that did not deter his willingness to speak to his friends, and he still prayed faithfully. Such an incredible example for us.

Further Questions for Study:

1) How do you feel about the expectation that it is the king's mandate and not the priest's mandate to evangelize and tell people about Christ?
   For you, is that surprising, nerve-wracking, or old news?

2) How much do you think Gnosticism (the belief that the world is evil, and spiritual acts are good) affects the way you view your job and your life?
   Why do you think that it is still so prevalent an idea today?

3) How confident are you feeling about sharing your faith, and telling someone about the gospel? If you're doing this book study with a group or friend, practice sharing your story with them now. If not, practice by writing it out.

Doubts, Fears, and Apologetics

*"When we communicate to the world about the God
they have yet to meet, it is essential that we communicate
light, life, and love."*
~Johnson/Valloton.

*"Christianity has not been tried and found wanting,
it has been found difficult and not tried."*
~G. K. Chesterton.

"I am the smartest person at my church." My friend turned and looked at me, exasperated. "At least sometimes, I feel like I am! Everything is 'just have more faith' and 'leave that topic for experts.' I went to school for eight years and have been trained to think, question, and understand logically. And at church, I'm ignored, or thought of as an unbeliever if I do? How is it faith—if it's totally blind?" My friend's husband hung his head, waiting for the reproach he figured he was about to get from me, too.

I blinked and took a deep breath, not sure how to answer. I honestly didn't feel like the smartest person at church, but I understood what he meant. At times, questioning and trying to think deeply about God is not encouraged, but discouraged in the church. I asked him to come to a Bible study for academic professionals, where we were wrestling with similar thoughts. He never came. What else could I have said, and what exactly did I believe myself?

In school we are taught to think deeply about the things we learn. We begin to approach everything from that way of thinking—understanding more, proving the hypothesis, talking through the possible options, strategizing what can come from it. But how does Christianity fit into this way of thinking?

Apologetics is defined as reasoned arguments, or writing in justification of something, usually regarding faith. I like the study of apologetics because it helps us learn how to appropriately think through our faith. Your average Christian doesn't study a lot of apologetics. Why bother studying a book written 2,000 years ago and act like it is applicable today—move on, right? God doesn't seem to have answers to most of our lives now. And if God isn't strong enough to handle our doubts and questions, is He worth studying about at all?

When I started college, I was uptight about getting my work done perfectly and looking like I had it all together. It was my identity, and I had to work hard to maintain it. So, a few months in as my friends started skipping classes, I refused to do so. Surely the teachers wanted us there, and even if attendance wasn't required, I was going to do the unexpected and be there every time. However, I was getting exhausted. Keeping up with class assignments, papers, volunteer work, friends—I was running around all the time. I was not a night owl, so waking up for 8 a.m. classes was initially not a problem; but as the year drug onward, I was struggling. Even though I was sleeping at night, I was no longer waking up when the alarm went off. So, I set another alarm. And then another one. Then I slept through a math class one morning where they spent the entire class talking about a difficult problem that I didn't understand. That was it for me—I made a vow I was going to make it to class somehow. I couldn't get to sleep any earlier, so I came up with a new plan I hadn't used in years—I was going to pray about it.

I had started going to my local campus ministry, and they were always harping on how important prayer was. I had stopped praying to God five years before, when my life had fallen apart in high school—but I needed some help, so I figured I would give it a try again. Besides, if God really was the God they were teaching about—surely, he could help me wake up!

So, I started praying every night before I went to bed that God would wake me up in the morning before class. I still set my alarms, and I still slept through all of them. But every morning, I started waking up just minutes before class started, with just enough time to actually get there. Now when I say waking up, this was unnatural, and every single day was different. For instance, I would feel the sunrise with its warm rays of light shining on my face—waking me up. Then I would open my eyes and realize that 1) the sun had already been up for hours, 2) the sunlight didn't ever shine through my window, and 3) because of the heavy blinds, the room was quite dark. Whatever, I was awake—time to go to class. God would surprise me in other ways. Once I was dreaming that I was doing homework with friends. My friend stopped me and said I wasn't supposed to be doing that right now. I responded, "What am I supposed to be doing?" He said, "Waking up for class." In that moment, I woke up, with minutes to spare. Some days, I just woke up. Others were fun surprises, but every night I prayed—and every morning, I woke up on time.

The whole "nightly experiment" sounds kind of absurd to me now. But after years of ignoring God, I was honestly trying to figure out whether or not He heard me. When that year finished, I *knew,* not only that could God *hear* me, but also that he *cared* about the things that mattered to me.

I spent the next few years mad at myself for having prayed so earnestly for such a trivial, selfish thing. Who in the world actually cared if I went to class or not? Nobody!

Except me.

And because it mattered so much to me, it mattered to God. God knew that the primary issue my freshmen year was not my perfectionism, but that I needed to have faith to trust Him again. He knew that responding to those prayers would give me a foundation in my faith. He knew that it would be something that I would carry always in my heart. Even now, when I am praying for something difficult, I think back to how patient and trustworthy and unchangeable God is, no matter what. God was faithful to help me build a foundation on Him, instead of myself.

I'm not suggesting you go out and test God. God knows where your heart is when you start to ask Him for things. My goal that year was not to test God, but to see Him.

If you honestly approach God with the aim to understand Him, He has the patience to take your craziness, and fears, and logicality— and give you something real in return.

He's not afraid of your questions and your insecurities. His name is not threatened by your desire to better understand. His position is not changed by your inability to see it. He would much rather you ask to know Him better, than to pretend that your unknowns don't exist. He would rather us tackle difficult questions with Him than run away from Him because of them.

My favorite pastor is a well-educated leader who has created a curriculum for how to think through our faith intellectually, as well as faithfully. He gives examples of his own personal struggles, "What if God was just a super-patient mastermind, and there is no heaven at the end of all of this?" That could make you sound like your faith is wavering if you stop there—or you can tackle the issue, instead of running away from it. You can study the character of God, understand that He is not an untrustworthy being, and come to the intellectual decision that whether there is a heaven or not, He is still worth it.

Thankfully God—the author of intelligence and thinking—can handle your questions. If He couldn't, He wouldn't be worth pursuing. Can anyone be too smart for a God who somehow had enough ingenuity, creativity, and intellect to create every flower, tree, atom, bird, color, mosquito, star, breeze, jaguar, mountaintop, quark, giraffe, snowflake, and person in the entire world? I want to follow a God who's smarter, wiser, more educated then I am! Because if He is not, I might as well just follow myself!

"The goal is not to survive intellectual challenges; the goal is to think critically and see how the Word

applies to every area of life, even academia."

So how do you tackle those doubts and complicated issues?

Don't be afraid of them. Questioning is how we learn. Anyone who has spent any time with a 4-year-old knows that a string of questions is coming, "What is that? Why did you do that? When can we go play? Why is the sky blue?" We learn by asking questions and struggling through the possibilities. We grew up by trying to understand the world around us, and likely made it through our careers so far by doing the same. But many of us may have stopped asking questions about God because they sounded like doubts. God is not afraid of your doubts. God is not afraid of your toughest philosophical, theological, scientific, or historical arguments. All doubts are based on assumptions *we* have, and often, if we work through our assumptions, we figure out the problems. If you trust God with them, you will get a lot farther in your faith than if you ignore them. *What good does it do to run away from something you will be encountering for the rest of your life?*

As a first-year medical student, I was in a Bible study with several older students who were ready to graduate. It was a wonderful group—they mentored us for our classes *and* faith. One day, we were all talking about the frustrating hours of classes, and one of the older girls said she never went to class! She exclaimed that she didn't want to be *indoctrinated* with all of the *other* things they taught. I had no idea what she meant. I loved class, so continued to attend, but I thought of her statement often. After a while, I was able to see what she meant. Teachers do not simply teach you the book knowledge you must know. Whether they mean to or not, they teach you their worldview—their beliefs, as well. It may be as subtle as an inflection, or as direct as telling us we wouldn't get anywhere without an additional degree after medicine. As you go through your studies, you will be exposed not only to what the books say, but also to the beliefs, expectations, and desires of the particular culture in which you work. When I started to realize all of the things that were being talked about in addition to medicine, I became concerned. What do you do with ideas you hear that do not fit in with your belief system? You can pretend they don't exist, or you can use them spur you on to better understand who God is.

With the rise of the Renaissance in history, many church leaders feared the knowledge the age brought with it. It brought questioning of the church, of the Bible, and of things that had been believed for years. But many of the Christian voices were not studying to disprove God, they were studying to understand the truths of the world and His Word. Knowing that God is wise and that He left us His Word, that can be studied and understood—they questioned, tested, and hypothesized in order to better know God. Studying and understanding the world around you does not have to divide you from God.

I read a book by an academic who purported that you make a decision to either believe God or believe the worldview—and you keep plowing through until you have the time to explore all the things you don't know and make them fit. About evolution he said, "In the meantime, I determined that my faith was based on realities that could stand by themselves, and that did not need to be subordinated to any explanation of science. Either I would discover that evolution was compatible with the God of my faith, or I would find that evolution was somehow wrong and I would stay with my faith." In short, he was unable to make it fit together, but still stuck firmly to his beliefs until he could figure out more. That is what I recommend to you about your own struggles. Don't bury them. Ask God to show you how to reconcile what you cannot see, and what you do not know...yet.

We cannot know everything. I cannot give you a scientific explanation of how Jonah was swallowed by a fish or where the Ark of the Covenant is now. I will search for some answers, but these two I have dropped! There are so many other things that solidify my faith that God is real, and I don't need these particular questions answered for myself. But I did need to research how reasonable it was that the Bible was legitimately copied and is the accurate Word of God. I know now and am confident. Some things you need to work through, and other things you will have to let go. Keep the main things the main things.

For answering questions, begin with a simple word search through the Bible. You won't find every answer to every specific question in your Bible, but you will be surprised by how much is actually covered. Did you know there's a verse in the Bible that actually says if you have a disagreement with your boss, do not quit your job? There's a reason I know that! Because I started looking in the Bible for examples of how to handle a stressful situation with my boss! Surely God would agree with me that this situation was wrong and I needed to leave—except the Bible clearly told me the exact opposite, and told me why.

Next, talk your questions through with Christians you trust. I have friends who tried to "explore their thoughts about God by themselves;" this more often leads to people giving up on their faith, rather than finding answers. It opens the door for confusion by the devil. People you talk with will not always have the answers, but the discussion will help you think through other aspects. The friend may have faced that same challenge already, and have ideas for how to approach it.

Also, with our technology, there are so many places to go online that discuss every aspect of Christianity. Caution— there are trustworthy sources, and those that are not. Check with your church and your mentors; and always pray for wisdom and discernment to know whether something is reliable. No matter what I am reading, even a trustworthy source, I filter everything through the Holy Spirit before taking it in as truth. If I am reading and start getting confused or uneasy, it is possibly not of God (the Holy Spirit communicates with me mostly through feelings of nervous anticipation).

Read everything with a grain of salt and a lot of prayer.

Lastly, accept that you will not get intellectually logical explanations for every question. "What exactly does heaven look like?" You aren't going to know here and now. When we reach those places of indecisiveness, we have to trust that 1) God knows the answers, and 2) God knows more than you do. One major thing that we lost with the age of enlightenment is our sense of humility. We assume that all things can be known, and that we can know it all! Why on earth should I trust a God that I am smarter than? Mostly, I trust God because I know that I am not smarter than He is. And, I accept that God is not going to tell me everything.

Even though our culture highly values knowledge, we do not know everything. There are multitudes of medical problems we do not understand, cannot fix, are limited in treating. We have only explored less than five percent of the ocean, which covers more than 70 percent of the planet's surface. There is so much about the world that we will never be able to know or understand. We are lacking all of the information, but God is all-knowing, omniscient. More importantly, He is good...there is no shadow of evil in Him. There are things that you will never be able to rationally understand in this life, yet you still need to be able to make a firm decision to trust God with your life. Those you evangelize will not be able to understand this at first, but they will respect it if you truly believe it.

Apologetics and Worldview

Apologetics is defined as reasoned arguments or writings in justification of something. It's a way we logically and rationally defend our faith. When you take the time to walk through questions to the faith that you have, this will help you when friends and coworkers have difficult questions. When you are talking to other people about their concerns, you do not need a seminary degree to answer their questions. Listen and hear the heart of what they are saying. Look at the worldview from which they are approaching God, and that will help you figure out how to respond.

In the worldview of my scientific friends, they think that the creation of the world needs a literal scientific explanation. They assume that the Bible is a scientific book written to explain how, why, and in what ways things have happened. That is a worldview—an expectation of books based on the world as they view it. Not all books are written that way (poetry books, or children's books leave a lot of gaps). The Bible is not written that way at all. Now, the creation of the world is a very popular topic, and godly scientists do have more specific explanations of the Genesis account. But overall, your goal would be to contrast the person's worldview with God's and describe how it may leave holes. Does their science book explain the origin of the universe in detail? What developed first to get from one cell organisms to two cell organisms? Thinking through it this way shows that both worldviews require faith to believe.

Apologetics reasoning 1) takes something that is known, 2) uses it to explain something that is not known about God, and 3) then leads into preaching the gospel. The Bible is written using the speech and culture of the known world of the listeners. In the parables, Jesus talks to the farmers and fisherman using stories, word choices, and processing that fisherman would understand. God teaches us within our own frame of reference; and that model is a way to teach others about God as well.

For my field, I like using the example of electrons. I took a class called organic chemistry—which is based on the study of electrons, the negative charge of an atom that can be passed around to create bonds that create new structures. The class is a study of how these electrons move. For all the time I have spent studying them, I have never seen an electron—I don't know for sure that they exist. I am told that there are electron microscopes, and multiple people have been able to personally see these supposed "electrons" and watch them move. And I've done experiments that suggest that electrons are working in a certain way to give me a physical result. But all I really have is the testimony of the scientists who have gone before me—who may just be *believing a massively complicated delusion!*

I know that's being dramatic, but here's the deal: I don't think about electrons and run off, assuming there is a huge conspiracy. Instead, I trust the word of those before me. I trust the position and books and eye-witness accounts of those scientists who did visually see and understand a process which I cannot personally attest to. In the same way, I believe the story of Jesus Christ. I believe the stories of the men who saw Jesus physically after the resurrection. There are many more extant manuscripts of the Bible, than of all the Greek philosophers combined. I believe the commands Jesus gave really do work—like "love your neighbor as yourself." There are eye-witness accounts, and books written, and great teachers for both electrons and Jesus. And I choose to believe them both—not because I have personally seen either one, but because I choose to believe they are true. Both take a tremendous amount of faith to believe, but I have not gone back on those decisions once. And the more I learn after that first step of faith, the more I believe.

Further Questions for Study:

1) What about for you?
   What do you see in your field that points you back to your relationship with God?

2) How could you use that to teach someone more about God?

Changing Our Leadership

Practice of the Presence of God

"Instead Christians should place a high value on all human work done by all people, as a channel of God's love for his world."
~Tim Keller

"Therefore, my beloved brothers, be steadfast, immovable, always abounding in the work of the Lord, knowing that in the Lord your labor is not in vain."
~1 Corinthians 15:58

After training, I went on several medical missions trips and was able to get connected with other pre-medical and medical students who joined us. I called Bianka a few months after a trip to see how things were going, since I knew she was going to be applying for med school soon. Bianka was a spicy, fun-loving Latina with a huge heart and a great gift for evangelism. She started telling me she was always on the lookout for how she could tell people about God. She was leading several Bible studies, volunteering half-day Sunday at church, a main leader in the campus ministry group, devoted to her own personal time with God, and had just started a new ministry project. I was getting overwhelmed just listening to her. She went on to tell me about all the science requirements and applications she was trying to complete as well. All of a sudden, I flashed back to when I was in school! Literally the only thing that had kept me from serving was if I was already committed to something else—and couldn't figure out a way to split my time to do both! I understood exactly what she was doing—because I had suffered through this fight—the fight between work requirements and ministry expectations.

I interrupted Bianka and reminded her that she was not in college to run a campus ministry by herself! She was there to learn the basic skills she would need to become a doctor. However—if she was going into full-time ministry—then she could continue on that path at that speed. But—if God had really called her into medicine—she was going to have to make some hard choices about her priorities. It's easy to feel like the only thing that matters to God is discipleship and evangelism. *But if God has placed you in the workplace, the most important thing he has for you to do is your job.*

You cannot spend every minute simultaneously serving at church, and getting your work done. Your primary focus and energy has to be put in the marketplace, and you need to commit to that and do your job well. When you do that, and continue listening to God, He will bring you the opportunities to serve in ministry as well—and you won't feel exhausted trying to run around doing both in your own strength.

Now, don't misunderstand me—this does not excuse you from serving in your church. This does not mean you can skip church services to do your homework. This does not mean you can ignore everything I just said about discipleship and evangelism. But it does mean that you have responsibilities to your studies and to your workplace, and you need to get those done and done well.

We cannot do our work instead of doing ministry; and we also cannot minister instead of doing our work.

In medical school, I failed a pharmacology test. The class teaches different medications and is primarily memorization. I failed for one simple reason—I wasn't doing my best. Why? I was in a band. Several of my classmates and I had formed what can best be described as an 80's cover band. Somewhere between volunteering at church, attending band practice, and just plain being lazy—I forgot the most important task that year—being a medical student! It was supposed to be my main goal, not my backup plan! Every time I put other things in front of it, I was playing games with my future.

More than that, I was doing work that was half-hearted, and unworthy of the calling that God had given me. I was no longer glorifying God with my work—I was just wasting my time. I had to refocus my many interests, put realistic boundaries on my time, and get down to business. God can easily work past imperfections, but it's much harder to work past a lackadaisical attitude. I had to give my whole heart to Him by producing my best work. It didn't matter what could have come of my misguided focus (my band had a couple of great shows!), either I was going to serve my current interest, or I was going to serve God and His. Which is it going to be for you? If everything you did was evaluated by the Lord himself, would you be proud of what you had done?

God is not a God of half-hearted and distracted work. God is a God of excellence. God didn't create the earth and say, "Well, I guess that's good enough!" He said, "It is good." The Creation Mandate in Genesis didn't say something like, "Spend your time focused on other things besides the job you're doing." We were given dominion over the earth because God entrusted us with the ability to make it fruitful, prosperous, and beautiful. That takes time and dedication. We cannot sacrifice the work God has given us to do in the workplace—for the mission God has given to us all.

I treat our mission of *ministry* as a *mindset* and *lens that I see through*— as I complete the *work* I have been given to do.

I read a book by a businessman who said he hated to hire Christians. He said often they were divided at heart—they were half-way devoted to serving God by ministering to coworkers, and half-way devoted to actually completing their work. How poor is your work ethic when your heart is not in what you do? You cannot be excused from doing your job because you spent several hours "at lunch" talking with someone about their salvation. You don't get exempted from workplace evaluations because you go to church on Sundays. You don't get a free ride and a life of perfect A's that you didn't have to study for, because God anointed you for your workplace. God isn't asking you to serve Him half-heartedly in two different venues. He isn't asking you to run around like a crazy person failing in different venues. He's simply asking you to focus on Him first, see things through His eyes, and let everything else fall into place.

If you put your workplace outcomes first, you'll never see the opportunities for ministry. If you put ministry first, you will be half-hearted and disrespected at the job God has given you. **But if you put Him first, all the other things will be added unto you.** He isn't asking anything of you but to serve Him with excellence in everything. He's there. Our goal is not in the grades, not in the outcomes, not in the strategies, it is the fully-committed heart. The goal is a heart that sees Him, working at a church, working in the marketplace, working with others. Then we can be ready to serve God in any way He chooses to use us.

Our work is not meaningless to God. The tasks we complete with our hands and minds glorify him. God's original plan was for us to explore, cultivate, and expand the world we were given. Our work has great value for our culture, and great value in worshipping Him.

I read a powerful book in medical school called *The Practice of the Presence of God.* It details how Brother Lawrence worked in a Carmelite monastery in Paris in the 1600's, and treated everything he did as an act of worship to God. He lived as if simple tasks like washing the dishes or baking bread were equal to spending hours in prayer with God. He had the ability to allow God into every aspect of his life. He used all of his life—whether working or not—to commune with, exalt, and spend time with God. He dedicated his actions so that they became acts of love toward God. He learned to turn his thoughts toward God, even when preoccupied serving someone else with all of his heart and mind. He knew God was near to him and that God was able to bestow grace, blessings, and His presence upon a person—

while they continued to do their work every minute of every day. People from all stations of life went to the monastery to learn from this humble servant of God.

I love the idea of being in constant communion with and worshiping God. Most of it comes down to the way that we think about the work we do. I made it my goal to practice the presence of God while I studied Anatomy. I learned to simply praise God while I studied the bones and muscles. I would think, "Wow, God you are so wise to have designed our arm with the muscles attached at these specific places. Thank you for designing me so excellently. Thank you for the pectoralis major and pectoralis minor which allow me to hug...." It actually changed studying into being time spent with God, that was enjoyable and flew by, rather than tedious.

Since then, I continue to look for God in the things I see every day. On my blog, for instance, I write about how I look for examples of Him in our jobs, in the culture we live in, and in what I study. I expect His presence and His help in the job I do. I expect to see Him, even in places where a person or a part of culture has completely rejected Him. I have honestly been encouraged by a dirty pan—but it's because I am always looking for hints of God, in everything I do. And I promise you—He's always there.

I expect God to help me see the problems in our culture, and also to point me to a solution. I love the story of Jesus and the disciples getting stuck on a boat during a storm, and Jesus sleeping through it. When they woke Him up to help, why were they surprised that Jesus could calm the water? We don't mind God working in the supernatural and at our church, but we tend to leave Him out entirely when it comes time to work in the natural—and all that does is limit what we ourselves are capable of—in the very places that need His intervention most.

Being able to focus on where God is—even when He is initially hard to see in some cultural situations—is what allows us to move forward redemptively. In your workplace, I assume you see much that is lacking, but there is also some good. There are some established themes in the world that do not follow God's guidelines, but because He is our creator, He ends up being written *in between the lines* in our cultures. For instance, when I see a movie or hear song lyrics that are unbiblical, I look for a message—not only the lies, but also for the hints of truth. When I practiced looking for God in a song, which physically did not react back at me—it helped me learn to react to people in my workplace—where emotions and frustrations sometimes clouded my ability to see the root of the problem. It is important to do this in our workplace, because we want to hold onto the truth, and redeem the lies that ruin our lives. How can we change anything if we don't see the problem?

Discerning the problem is sometimes the hardest part. For example, the creation of the hospital was because of Christians. They were the ones who originally taught that God valued every human being, and that God could heal from disease. This was unlike the culture of their time. It was Christians who wanted to serve that created a place where the sick would be fed and watched over. They looked at the culture and saw hurting people who were being ignored, and they intervened.

Perhaps we can discern a problem that today's culture is crying out about, and inject life and redemption where there is little or none. It's this same way of thinking that fought against infanticide, that eventually abolished slavery, that created the social justice missions movement we have now. We don't always get things right as a church, so don't get distracted right here! What things are happening in your field, in your job, in your workplace that are not of God that could possibly be redeemed? It's spending time with God, listening to what the cultural problems are, and asking God for His redemptive heart, that gives you the ability to take that step to begin to change the things that weigh on you.

Working in a hospital can be very disheartening. There are people who are treated and sent home healthy, but many others who are not. It is frustrating that families and patients are usually scared or angry, and often take it out on those caring for them. In response, practitioners create a wall, or thick-skin, in order to continue caring for their patients, in spite of their negative reactions and difficult situations. This defensive coping mechanism also usually causes practitioners to react by making fun of the situation, instead of crying about it. It helps us get by. But it hurts my heart when people on my team insult patients in jest. If I hear it happening, I often try to verbally and calmly help rethink the situation. "Yes, that mother was yelling obscenities at you, I'm sorry, but let's remember her child has an undiagnosed medical problem and mom is terrified. We need to be patient with her".

If we can rethink the way we talk about a situation it can change the way we react to it. In fact, I was able to get several mothers who were angrily refusing procedures to get on the same page as the team, simply because I did not view them as "heinous obstructions to healthcare," as the team was joking that morning. Another time, this viewpoint helped me understand that the parents' family member had recently died from a simple procedure that we needed to do on their child. It took more time and patience than usual, but I was finally able to help them understand that their child was not going to die, and we were able to treat the child. The "name-calling" bothers me, not because I'm "holier than my coworkers," but because I asked God for the opportunity to see what He sees, while I'm at work. That is something God put on my heart as an opportunity to redeem that which had been lost. *God loves people even when they yell at me.* No, I didn't change the whole warped health care system because of that, but that day I did get to change what happened for that patient and for our team. And I'll take that. God can redeem anything that seems lost and deplorable, if we will just let Him participate.

I worked for a while at a clinic struggling with multiple issues. No one had told the patients that their old pediatrician was leaving. Patients would come in angry, "That's not how the old doctor did it." The nurses couldn't stand the administrative staff and vice versa! In addition, the management blamed me for not having expert marketing and managerial strategies to fix it all! It was insane, and I felt like I had no power to solve any problems at all.

In retrospect, when the clinic closed down, I realized that I had what might have been the perfect opportunity to step in with the power and presence of God, and to redeem that which was dying—but I never took it. My excuses were legit—*I was the new doctor... the situation was unfair... the management did this... and I was busy....* But in reality, God had anointed me as a Christian in the marketplace with the ability to reshape the environment, influence the culture, and change the sphere of problems I saw—but I didn't do it. I threw out the entire situation as hopeless—instead of focusing on the one area under my influence. It's one thing to say I *understand* the mission of God, but another thing entirely to *live* it.

Kingdom-minded Christians desire to redeem not just hearts, but products, services, opportunities, environments, and lives. Because treating our work as worship to God sometimes only makes tiny advances, but it has the power to create a community that loves and redeems a fallen world. It has the power to anoint us to offer real solutions to the things we see every day. It has the power to unite with the efforts of the local church, and change lives. Our very actions can be worship to God. Our very thought life can glorify God. And our daily work can lift Him up, whether it's considered "ministry" or not. But in order for any of that to happen, I have to be at my job, fully engaged, working with excellence, fully listening to God, and willing to step out when He says go—whether "go" means changing the way my team thinks, or telling someone about Christ. Are you taking the chances you have to do so?

Ecclesiastes 3:12-13, *"I perceived that there is nothing better for them than to be joyful and to do good as long as they live; also that everyone should eat and drink and take pleasure in all his toil—this is God's gift to man."*

Further Questions for Review:

1. Currently, are you more likely to overlook work or overlook opportunities to minister? What would it take to change that?

2. What would it take to put God in first place in both your work and ministry?

3. What if the best part of your job was not the coming paycheck but the very work you did every day? What might that look like for you?

4. What environment do you work in? Performance-oriented and fear-based? One without vision or opportunities for advancement? One without order and structure?

5. "You have the ability to change the environment." How are you doing at it?

Imago Dei

"God calls us first to a person—himself.
Then you are called to a purpose— to become like Him."
~Chip Ingram

"You can always tell the size of a man's identity
by the size of the problem it takes to discourage him."
~Karl Valotten

"Remember that you are unique.
If that is not fulfilled, something wonderful has been lost."
~Martha Graham

I pulled out the lists I had made and looked through them one more time. Something had to be missing. There must be more activities that I had simply forgotten about. And there had to be more mentors who could write references. This couldn't be it. Or more literally, if this was it, I was screwed. I was never going to get into medical school.

My junior year of college, when filling out applications for medical school, I came to a sudden identity crisis. The activities I had done throughout college did not suggest that I was about to become a doctor. I did volunteer once with a doctor, but it was the only activity outside of class that had anything to do with medicine at all. My interests were not at all what the premedical courses had recommended. I don't remember how, but I subconsciously decided that instead of doing what they told us, I was just going to be myself.

Amazingly enough, that translated into me choreographing a Filipino dance, being treasurer for an after school program, singing worship at our campus ministry group, writing poetry, and working as a bank teller. It was a long weird list, but only one out of a dozen things had anything to do with medicine. When I realized that, my palms started to sweat. The only kind of doctor I was setting myself up to be was a frenzied one with an identity crisis. Where I spent most of my time spoke loudly of where my heart was, and it seemed to be nowhere near medicine.

In addition, I had spent the last few months studying for the MCATs, and it wasn't going well. I had A's in all my science classes, but putting everything together at the same time wasn't as easy. I started to worry I wasn't cut out for medicine, and these struggles were telling me to give up and try something else.

Luckily, I had a backup plan. Really, it should have been my initial plan, but a minor detail! My backup plan was to ask God. It was time for the annual student conference, so I took the weekend off and headed out, ready for some serious encouragement, and probably redirection into some other job. Like I said, I had been terrified for several years that if I actually asked God what he wanted me to do, he was going to tell me to give up college and go be a missionary in the middle of nowhere. So, I figured I was finally here—this was the time for God to tell me to forget studying and to enter ministry.

Imagine my surprise when the main focus of the conference was "that God calls and anoints people to work in the marketplace." The entire weekend I felt like God was telling me he was going to use all of the random interests I had, and I was going to become a doctor unlike anything I'd seen before. I went back to school energized and excited to receive the miracle I'd been praying for—passing my test with flying colors. But there was no miracle to help me pass the test, I did exactly as I expected—poorly (I'm being slightly dramatic—I did average). And suddenly, everything that it seemed like God had promised seemed completely impossible.

I theoretically knew what the requirements were to be considered a good candidate. Studies show that the average pre-medical student who is well rounded is more likely to succeed in the high-stress situations schools place you in. But they didn't just want well rounded—they wanted a clear interest and dedication to science and medicine. But I questioned every recommendation. If I spent eight hours in class, couldn't I also spend an hour or so dancing and still become a doctor? Why did it matter so much if I fit into their mold or not? Why couldn't I just make my own?

My adviser instructed me to apply to different schools, insisting that my alma mater was not going to accept me. But months later when the applications were due, I decided to send them in anyway. God had told me I was going to be a doctor, and maybe someone out there wanted an oddball? I sold my random interests for all I could, and waited.

And you know what happened? A miracle I never even prayed for. I was accepted at one of the top medical schools in the country, and offered a full-ride scholarship. When God wants you somewhere, He will provide the way.

But the other thing that it taught me, was that it was okay for me to be me.

Often we end up limiting ourselves to a title or job description. People define what is acceptable for a position, and everything else is considered outside those parameters. But we can't spend our lives trying to fulfill someone else's expectations.

One of my favorite things to study is identity. People have thought me weird, odd, and crazy my whole life. I'm not really strange—it's because they can't fit me into the boxes that so many others are categorized by. Learning about identity gives me hope that in spite of my *craziness*, I am not a chemical bottle that God accidentally spilled on the floor and messed up the original plan. He specifically made me not to fit in the box. **I was created just to be me.**

We as a culture are not great at finding identity. Children ask "Why?" Then teens begin to ask, "Who am I?" to search for answers. Because we as humans are so bad at answering this question, we tell people to experience a variety of activities, and thus find their identities as they go. We don't really mean that they will find their identity, we mean they will find activities that they can use to define themselves.

But the Bible says that we were created in the image of God. Each one of us reflects God in one unique, singular way. We were created by the Creator who named billions of stars, so His creativity is unlimited. We are all perfectly unique in and of ourselves—but if we spend our time trying to become like someone else, we become counterfeit copies — not ourselves at all. **You were created to just be you.**

I went to Monteverde, Costa Rica years ago and went on an incredible zipline—flying over the jungle. It was quite intimidating—I'd never done anything like that before. It was really fast and over a mile in the air. I choked back my fear and did it anyway—because the first person in line was a five-year-old boy who was not scared. I couldn't let him show me up, so I had to make it happen—even jumping off of ledges on Tarzan swings! I struck up a conversation with the boy and asked him what he wanted to be when he grew up, thinking he would want to work on the zip-line with the other young, adventurous guys employed there. Do you know what he told me? He wanted to stack suitcases at the airport. Now, to be fair, that is a very creative career goal for a five-year-old, and somebody does need to stack suitcases! But for a five-year-old who thinks flying in the air in the jungles is easy—is it possible he might be able to dream of something a bit more adventurous, because of who he is?

First we need to know ourselves and our abilities, and then we need to choose our work.

You were created to be just you. God told me one time that He wouldn't love me any less if I sat on the couch for the rest of my life. Now He could afford to tell *me* that—I'm an overachiever that can't make it more than a day or two of just sitting around. But the point was clear—although the world may measure me by what I can do, produce, prove, or obtain—my worth in God is not dependent on any of those things. It is dependent on Him—and because He is unchanging and all-loving, it's a pretty great place to be. In the real world, the fact that your value comes from your actions is not always stated, but it is implied, if you read *in between the lines* of applications, reviews, and articles. But regardless of the worldly measure that may be used, we need to keep our eyes focused on God, and the gifts He has given us— knowing that if we trust in Him, He will take care of everything else.

New Name/New Identity

Of course, I can't learn anything well the first time, so this couldn't be the end of the chapter. It took me years to realize that the problem with my medical school applications wasn't my extra-curricular activities —*it was that I had not defined my identity*. God had told me that I was going to be a doctor unlike anything I had seen before. So I treated it like a mandate. I was going to study like this, talk like this, and walk like this. I completely missed the point for many years: God didn't give me direction in order to give me a heavy burden. God was giving me a new name.

I had spent most of my life known by what I did: straight-A student, the triple-threat, do anything, super-smart multitasker. But I was running myself ragged trying to keep up with all the things people expected me to be. As I became a doctor, I added more things: I had to be the confident, well spoken, restrained person with wise words, and an empathetic but not emotional attitude. I was doing a ton: working part time as a pediatrician, part time as a medical missions director, leading Bible study, taking leadership seminars at the church, studying for medical accreditation exams, and working seven days a week trying to fit it all in, yet always behind. I was discipling, evangelizing, leading, working, and serving. But isn't this what God meant? He was Lord, and I was going and doing.... Yet...Not long after—I seriously crashed. I quit my job, finished up the trips for the year, and sat at home, confused. If this was really what God wanted from me, I didn't want any more of it. I wasn't going to make it another day, let alone 30 plus more years! I was exhausted— I was done.

I glumly reviewed all the things I had written in my journal that God had said I should do. I reviewed books I had taught about work. I prayed and fasted and begged God to tell me what I was supposed to do next, because I couldn't sit at home "recovering" forever—my savings account was going to run out soon. And mostly I just dreaded what I assumed was coming, "Ashley go back and do all the same things I told you to do. Use the gifts I gave you— and stop complaining!"

But somehow that didn't sound like God, that sounded more like me. It was many months of soul-searching before I finally figured out the problem—which was, of course, *me*.

In the Bible, God often started a journey for people by given them a new name. Abram and Sarai he changed to Abraham and Sarah. Saul was changed to Paul. My name was still Ashley, and I figured it was going to stay that way. But the reason God changed people's names was in order to give them a new identity, and sometimes that was more in theory than in actual name. Gideon was taken from "lowest of the lowest of the lowest" to "courageous soldier." Peter went from "the listener" to "the Rock I will build my church on." He gave people a new way to see and think about themselves—which may have been different from what everyone else saw or expected. Often the name and the goal came at the same time, like with Peter. But the important thing was that Peter was not called a rock and instructed to build a church because of his new name, he was re-named as the Rock, and then allowed to help God build a church (Matthew 16:17-18). It's a very narrow, but very important distinction. We are not getting the name *if* we perfectly work out God's mandate, we are renamed whether we do it perfectly or not at all. We are not what we do, we are God's.

It's easy to say. But something entirely different to believe and live. *You are not what you do.* Even for those who have been given the gifts and the talents, the opportunities, or a clear call into a field, God does not mean for that to be a burden for you. He means for it to be an opportunity for you. But before you go, or do, or build—you have to get one thing straight—where your identity truly comes from.

In medicine, a new real identity emerges as you advance in your profession. One night you're a worthless student, and then at graduation, a piece of paper puts you in charge. It leaves everyone wondering where this new identity came from overnight. So even if I tell people, "Just call me Ashley," they won't do it! They always use the term "Doctor." It's a new identity that I have been given that determines where I go, how I see myself, and how others see me. But if that's all I limit myself to see, that's all I will ever be.

But God tells us, "You are his masterpiece, created perfectly in His image to do what He planned in advance for you to do." Our name comes first, our tasks second. You can't reverse it, or you will end up exhausted, overworked, and bitter at the task-driver, who you assume to be God. God is not a task-driver. He loves you. Loved you before you ever chose a field. Loved you when you failed that test, broke that confidence, messed up that opportunity, or ignored His direction. Loved you when people called you crazy, stupid, insignificant, or purposeless. Loved you when you hated yourself. Loved you when you hated Him. Loved you the days you perfectly read your Bible and attended church, and just the same on the days you stayed home doing nothing. Loves you in and out every day, no matter what, and will never, ever stop. Perhaps this is all a little too mushy for a book for business/medical/academic people, but it's so true I couldn't brush past it. He loves you not because of what you do each day, but in spite of it. The only way to make it without burning out is to get the order straight: 1) We are loved and valued by God just as He made us, and 2) We have a job to do.

Imago Dei

Imago Dei is a Latin phrase meaning *Image of God*. Genesis 1:26-27 starts with God saying, "Let us make man in our image, after our likeness. And let them have dominion... So God created man in his own image, in the image of God he created him, male and female he created them." The word used there for "image of God" is "tselem" which means "reflection or image of something greater."

It means He made us, from the get-go, to be like Him. It means that from the beginning of time we were created, anointed, and blessed to be His ambassadors, His representatives, and His right-hands here on earth. It's an incredible honor.

God made us in his image. That means we have value. Value that came not because we were the smartest, or had the best resume, but value that came because He was a part of us. Value that cannot be blemished, cannot be discarded, and cannot be broken. You have great worth and God knows it. Do you?

It's not value that comes from hitting all your "perfect Christian expectations." On some level, I made it through my training because I broke some of my own expectations for myself. I went to church post-call in scrubs instead of dressed up perfectly because otherwise I would have missed the entire service! I committed to go places or do things that were for God and not for my resume. I dedicated myself to Christian friendships and sometimes that meant I would help them set up for a party I couldn't actually go to, just to spend time with them! I sometimes probably looked crazy. But I did what I had to do to get around people who were going to remind me that my worth didn't come from how good my grades were and how well I finished that last project. Your value in Christ cannot be diminished, no matter what. And you need to take the time to remind yourself of that regularly as you go.

We have a mission. The mission does not determine whether or not God cares about you, or gives you the time of day. He is not an evil boss hovering over you, He is a proud father, giving you what is His to take care of and improve on, because He trusts you. These two points must be understood. You are God's. He trusts you with much. Do you believe that?

Or do you believe what people have told you all your life? Do you believe the circumstances you were in, more than you believe you are God's? Do you believe the lies and limitations others have placed on you, or that you have believed yourself? You are His. You are forgiven, you are anointed, you are empowered, and you are God's. This is a foundation you need to believe, as you go forth walking out the things He has called you to do.

I spent many years seeing myself as a prisoner—stuck in my own limits and decisions and prisons of self-doubt and perfectionism. It was years before I realized that God had long before let go of that image of me, and saw me as His royal daughter and confidant. If God has not yet given you a new name, or a new image of who you are, spend some time right now praying, and asking Him to re-write who you are and how you see yourself.

And then spend some time for the next few weeks confessing it. I spent many years responding to my own self-doubt and fears with the simple proclamation, "No, I am His." That means I am a child of God. I am chosen, I am sanctified, I am justified, and I am more than a conqueror, not because of anything I can do, but because of everything that Christ did for me. I was remade from my former mistakes, problems, limits, and issues, into what God intended for me from the very beginning. I am not who I was. I am His. And that is more than good enough for all that God has called me to do.

Further Questions for Study:

1) Spend some time praying right now.
   If God hasn't ever given you a new name/identity, ask him for one right now.
   If he has, review what God has told you.

2) Pray the last paragraph above out loud—what does it mean for you to declare, "I am His?"

3) How have you seen your career determine your identity in life, instead of the opposite?
   How can you make sure you keep your priorities straight?

Foundations

*"You can't build a dream or a business or a career on a gift.
You build it on character. And that takes time and energy
to build... People don't fail from lack of information,
they fail from lack of character."*
~Jossy Chacko

*"Even when it is not well with our circumstances,
it can be well with our souls."*
~Jennifer Rothschild

A tuba solo interrupted the silence and filled the room—I just smiled. I never knew what I was going to hear through the walls of the dorm, but I was starting to enjoy it. In my sophomore year of college I shared an incredible apartment/dorm with nine of my friends from the college ministry group. We ladies had our own kitchen, bathrooms, ten bedrooms, and a large family room. Even cooler, ten of our guy friends from the ministry lived next door. I shared a thin wall with Eric. Most of the time, he was pretty quiet. Every once in a while he would go off on his tuba for an hour, or listen to some worship music. But my favorite thing was sometimes in the morning when he was getting ready for class, I could hear him boldly and loudly reading Bible verses.

Our ministry was big on the power of confessing Scripture out loud. Any event we went to, we would get lists of verses for different topics: to believe for healing, to fight spiritual battles, or to remind us of our identity in Christ. We were told that we just needed to read the verses out loud for ten minutes a day, and stick with it, for them to be effective. I intended to read them but usually forgot, talked myself out of it, ignored their importance—basically, I just didn't do it. But almost every morning, Eric did.

I didn't think much of it, until somewhere near the end of the year, when I realized that he was a completely different person. Eric had started off a young Christian, still trying to figure out his life, his faith, and his involvement in church. He ended the year a confident man of God, and a respected leader of our ministry. I had never been more surprised at how a single year could change a friend's life so completely. Even more than that, until then, I had not realized how big of a deal a strong foundation in your faith really is.

I spent the next several years reading verses aloud in the morning, as faithfully as I could, but without that same impact. To be fair, he was doing more than reading verses—he was faithfully going to church, letting mature Christian men mentor him, was involved in a Bible study, studying and believing the Word, and spending time with God through prayer. You could see the foundations he laid by the end of that year. I so appreciated that our campus ministry had taught us about doing simple but necessary things, like quiet time, in order to lay strong foundations for a firm and unmoving belief in God.

Initially, I thought working on our foundations as a Christian was just a timing thing—similar to the way I studied for classes. Ten minutes studying equaled a certain grade—but ten hours studying equaled one much better. What I learned was, the important thing was not how long I spent, what exactly I did, or even how many times I confessed verses. The important thing was the commitment to making God a part of my day before anything else. The important thing was the commitment to build my faith and my security and my confidence, not on the hours I was studying—but on the moments I spent at God's feet. The important thing was not whether I was reading, or praying, or shouting—but that my heart was dedicated to getting to know God better, and in the process, getting to know me better as well.

I started medical school terrified with the thought of spending 60 hours a week with people who were angry, confused, ungodly, and sometimes just plain evil. I did not want to end up looking like them. How was I supposed to spend my days experiencing anything but God, and still stay a respectable Christian? I finally realized that God doesn't add things up like we do. In many training programs, you have to hit 1,000 supervised hours to be considered legitimately trained. God calls brand new Christians to speak His name, change lives, and perform miracles. Most schools require certain prerequisites before allowing anyone to advance. God only asks for a prayer, and gives us the world. Graduate training requires multiple degrees and crazy tests to move anywhere within our fields. God simply requires a willing heart. He doesn't add up our worth by how many hours, and list requirements we have completed. He already gave us our worth, and nothing we do can change that. Our actions are not a list of resume requirements, nor ways to get on the Boss' good side. They are a thank you, and a response to an incredible gift. So, we don't need to add them up—we just have to trust and follow Him.

Every year of college, medical school, and residency looked different for me from a growing foundations perspective. One year I took leadership classes at the church that involved hours of study. One year I barely made it to church—on call almost every Wednesday and Sunday night. One year I led the worship team at my college. But most years I barely got to sing at all. One month I would wake up early and spend time before work studying the Bible. The next month I would be unable to push back my 4 a.m. alarm any more, and would read at night instead. Every year and month was different in terms of exactly what it looked like. But every day, and every month, and every year, I made a pledge to find time to build Christian foundations inside of me.

Maybe this year for you won't include 4-hour devotional studies at church. Maybe it won't be you leading the study or volunteering every day at church or spending 2 hours a day in prayer. But could your year involve you spending ten minutes speaking truth out loud while you do your hair? Could your year involve you reading a scripture off of a note card in your coat pocket, every time you have a bathroom break? Could your year involve you praying while you drive to and from work? Could your year involve you and your friends emailing encouraging prayers and verses to each other? It's not hard to find the time when you view it the same way you prioritize your studying, your research, and your career. But you have to make it a priority.

The Reason for Foundations

My life is a testament, if nothing else, about how far those foundations can take you. In residency, after I had meningitis, even the simplest of things became a chore. I was a good resident, but mostly because I checked my work four times, every time. I got to work an hour earlier than anyone else so I had enough time to do so. And I worked on notes the night before. I had to put in a lot of time to end up at the same level of "keeping it all together" as my fellow residents. Most of the time, my memory, my concentration, my understanding wasn't up to the perfect standards, if I didn't put in more extra time than everyone else. Because I was working so hard to do my job, I basically stopped trying to encourage, or disciple, or evangelize the people around me. I didn't even try to befriend them. I had a job to do, and that was my main priority for most of the three years. As I neared the end, I started to lament the time I had lost. Maybe I could have tried harder, but my life was focused on survival. I didn't talk much about my illness or my faith, and figured this part of my life would just go down on the books as largely pointless. But one day I got a phone call in the midst of a crazy morning that changed my mind.

Down the hall people were yelling; the commotion and carts headed in that direction told me that one of the patients was coding—critical. My heart started pacing nervously—I hated codes! In my state, I could barely think through one thing at a time, let alone multiple crises. I saw the attending and another doctor run past the windowed work room where I was, I didn't follow, knowing the situation was covered. The phone in the room started ringing; my pager began going off, and now the code pager buzzed as well. I reached to press the button to stop the incessant buzzing when the other call pager started rattling in its clip at my hip. Seriously? Shouts still echoed off the walls down the hall, but nothing that sounded like they needed me to intervene. What was I going to do anyway? I couldn't even remember patients' names, let alone what I was supposed to be doing, before the phone and pagers started their incessant calls. I reached down to pick up the phone as the second telephone in the room started ringing. Was that seriously four pages and two calls I had just missed in 30 seconds?

"Hello..." Oh man, where was I? What was the name of this part of the hospital? The NICU? No, these were the big kids... I couldn't remember, forget it—stick with what I know. "Hello, this is Ashley" was all I could manage. I dropped a pager and it went scurrying across the floor. On the other end of the phone line, one of the first-year fellows called out, "Ashley, it is always so great to talk to you! You are always so calm and collected."

I stood annoyed, trying to hold the phone between my ear and shoulder and using the other hand to reach in my back pocket and pull out the sheet about the patients that she would be calling while the other land line in the room incredibly started ringing yet again. I sat confused for a second thinking, "Calm"?!? Where did she see "calm"? I was literally shaking! I could barely think straight, let alone be calm about anything in the midst of the incessant paging, dying patients, and never-ending work. Honestly, I couldn't even remember the person's name that I was talking to, though I recognized her voice. But I guess in my voice she had heard something that not even I could identify at the moment, "a peace which passes all understanding," no matter what is going on. A peace that didn't come in that moment, or that morning, or even that year. A strength that didn't come from me, and that I honestly didn't even see myself. A foundation of peace that had been laid down years before, that had never left me, no matter how bad it got.

The Tendency with Foundations

I once worked on the psychiatric ward and saw patients with significant illnesses. But my first admit was the most perplexing to me. He was a clean-cut young man about my age, in a polo shirt and khakis, dressed very similar to people I had gone to college with. We had good conversations about his healthy lifestyle, his favorite books, his aspirations when he finished college in a few months. He seemed so normal, at some point I honestly forgot that he was a patient in the psychiatric hospital. He clearly explained that he had been having headaches that were interfering with his schoolwork, that medications were not working, and he was there to figure out how to get rid of the problem.

I went back and talked to my attending, very confused—reporting that he seemed like a normal healthy college student who was having headaches. The attending gave me the results of his MRI, sent me back in to talk to him. I explained that everything looked great on the MRI, and there were no signs of any structural abnormality or dangerous lesions to explain his headaches, but surely we could find something to help control them.

The young man replied, "But what about the chip?"

"The—the chip?" I stammered back, confused.

"The government put a chip in my head and that's what's causing the headaches. I know it's on the imaging somewhere—surely you can see the chip on the MRI, right Ashley? Please, tell me you can see the chip so we can get it removed, so they will stop watching me!"

I am honestly still disturbed by it. He looked perfectly normal, but was believing a powerful delusion, that there was a chip implanted in his brain that was not actually there. It had not destroyed his life at that point, but was in the process of starting to do so. I later found out he had recently been kicked out of college. Even more disturbing—he easily could have been me. If he had not been admitted to the hospital, we could have been good friends. But the mind is a powerful instrument that can distort, confuse, and destroy the very lives we've built—even the logic and wisdom that we far too often stand on.

We have to make it a point and a goal in our lives to keep foundations in Christ our main focus before any problems arise.

We cannot go by what we feel, or think, or fear, or hate. We have to go by the Word of God. Foundations are the compass that tell us if we are flying straight and doing well, or if we are slowly but surely heading for a horrible crash.

We all know stories of people who showed great promise, did incredible things, and then fell from great heights, due to sin. Conversely, some Christians remove themselves from the culture where we were given the responsibility and the ability to change. They avoid anything that is not church-related, shut off all non-Christian influences, and stay as far away as possible from anything not-of-God. But since it is our mandate to work in the secular world, we cannot run away from everything; we need to know our own weaknesses and avoid temptation from those those things that can distract us.

I have never smoked or done drugs, so I am not tempted by them. But, I have a huge sweet tooth, and some crazy strange eating habits when stressed. So, even on an awful day, if you put me on the set of *Breaking Bad*, I wouldn't be tempted by drugs. However, if you put me in the middle of Krispy Kreme on a bad day, it is possible I might eat my own weight in donuts. I know myself well enough to know that desserts would take me out before drugs! We cannot dismiss our own weaknesses, we need to be aware of them, as well as to be aware of our possibilities.

You've likely spent time dreaming about what could be possible if you get your degree, get that job, take on that project, or accomplish that goal. How much time have you spent thinking about who you would be once you got there? Where would your tendencies take you, if you got everything you ever wanted? What weaknesses are you ignoring, that the devil would prey upon? What sins in your life, if left unchecked, could slowly eat away and destroy your career?

Even as we have studies, and goals, and things God has told us to do, His ultimate goal is our hearts set and planted on Him. It doesn't matter how great and impressive we look, if we are falling apart on the inside. We will only make it so long before the lies, confusion, and insecurity will take out our impressive image—and our life, also. **Only standing on God gives us the ability to stay on a true course for the things we believe about ourselves and and about God.** We can easily get distracted by the pain we see, the harsh reality of life, and the things that come up that didn't go according to plan. Or we can keep standing on God's foundations—both when things are great, and when they are lacking.

It took me awhile to realize that although I had spent a lot of time working on foundations in my life, I was thinking of them in the wrong way. Your foundations do not give you right standing in this world right now, they give you the truth to stand on, whether things go great or go haywire. You can't stand on them as goals you've "accomplished" that deserve a great payout. I used to add up a list of my own works and accomplishments, and wait for the due respect, security, and money that should come from what I did! But life is not a box of chocolates, and God is not a vending machine. All that I have was given to me, and none of it gives me any identity, any respect, or any credit at all.

Real foundations get you to a point where you are not feeling entitled for decisions and choices you made—you are being thankful for the decisions God already made.

They take you back to the reality of who God is, and who He anointed you to be—not the other way around.

Most importantly, Foundations are what make you a leader worth following. Great leaders don't fall when their life doesn't go the way they expect. They get frustrated, then they refocus and get back to possibility. Great leaders don't change their mind every week about what the vision is and how they will get there. Great leaders don't work for a week and then give up on everything if it hasn't panned out in the positive. Great leaders know how to stand through the trial and the storms and the elation and their weaknesses, because they don't stand on themselves—they stand on God. And thankfully, in God's kingdom it's not about how great your resume looks, or how many wins you made, or how perfect your dream is, or how many tribulations you fought through— all God needs to use someone for greatness is a willing heart. He's done it for me, so if you haven't seen it yet in your life, hang in there, focus on foundations, and just trust Him to do the rest.

Hebrews 10:35-36, 39 "Therefore do not throw away your confidence, which has a great reward. For you have need of endurance, so that when you have done the will of God you may receive what is promised.... But we are not of those who shrink back and are destroyed, but of those who have faith and preserve their souls."

Further Questions for Review:

1) How are you doing making foundations a priority in your life?

2) What role have you seen foundations play in your work so far?

3) How do you practically concentrate on foundations in your spiritual life while still being excellent at your career requirements?
   What does that look like in your life right now?

Fear and Failure

"There is no failure in Christ."
~Dr. Tyler Cooper

"Shame is the sense of having lost value as a person
because of mistakes, failures, or rejection."
~Gist. Michael Anderson

*O*migoodness, here it is! An email from the American Board of Pediatrics. All that waiting, but it is finally here! And after failing the past two years... never mind, no need to think about that right now. Here is your letter of redemption! I nervously clicked on the opening link, and simultaneously tried to look and not look at the same time.

But the message was clear very quickly. "We regret to inform you, that you have failed the examination." It went on to say something else about something else, but what else mattered? I had failed.

Not once. Three times. Over 1,000 hours of studying. Thousands of practice questions. A trip out of state to an elite, reputable review for a week of non-stop, information-overload. $10,000 down the drain. I had meticulously followed the schedule to the last painful detail—reviewing pictures, topics, questions, vaccinations, complications—and then started to review it again. I had put in the time. I had put in the energy. And this time—I went in fighting spiritually as well! I prayed every time before I studied. I had verse after verse that I proclaimed and memorized and meditated on. On a practical level, I had done everything right. I

149

had gotten a time extension, due to my history of brain damage. I had quit my job so that I had two months without work, so I could study full-time this year. And—I prayed to God for a miracle— since my effort alone clearly wasn't doing the trick. But all of that was not enough. After all the strategizing, time, energy, and prayer—I still failed. Not once, not twice, but three times!

A heaviness weighed down my body, and tears blurred the painful truth on the screen. How was I supposed to be the doctor God had told me to be, even when I had asked Him, "Will you help me do it," but the answer still seemed to be no? What on earth was I supposed to do now?

When I initially started writing this book, the story above was the conclusion. I went on to say something about "how even though I failed my career, I hoped you would succeed at yours." My mom chastised me for being so defeatist, so I changed the conclusion completely. But I didn't want to drop this story, because as awful as it was for me, and as much as I hope you will all succeed at everything you do, I know some of you will fail. Fail while doing the right thing. Fail while doing your best. Fail while standing and working exactly where God told you to be. And as grotesque as it sounds, failure makes us better—but only when we understand and react to it appropriately.

I was surrounded by people who were high achievers. It wasn't enough to get the best marks on that rotation, this person was training for a marathon as well. It wasn't enough to get a medical degree, this person was adding other degrees as well. If this person failed the test or need remediation, it was swept under the rug and no one ever spoke of it again, unless in hushed tones, like some horrible family secret. I saw that pattern throughout grad school— perfection was expected and glorified, while mediocrity, or *gasp* failure was intolerable. *I never recall anyone talking about what it was like to reach the end of their ability, and make a mistake. And more than that, I never recall anyone teaching me how to deal with it if I did.*

I didn't know how to help myself after finishing residency when I could not pass our final accreditation exams. I am a doctor and practice in the US, but the test must be passed in your first seven years after finishing your training, or you have to start residency over again entirely. That wasn't an option for me after having been sick the first time—I refused to repeat any of that! So, I sat, looking in frustration at my pathetic medical career—11 years of preparation, service, loans, and time—to get to the end and walk away empty handed?

My thoughts went in crazy circles I couldn't seem to control. What if I wasn't smart enough to pass? What if meningitis really did destroy my brain and I would never pass? Was this a sign I just didn't need to work as a doctor? How many times should I fail before I gave up and tried a new venture? And more importantly, if God could help me every single day to see patients, to pray for miracles, to redeem the culture around me—why on earth couldn't or wouldn't He help me here?

I blamed myself, the test, the books, and even the couch I studied on. But that got me nowhere. I got depressed and hopeless. I couldn't bear to take the test again—I didn't even believe I could pass it, what was the point of trying? I took a year off, aimlessly trying to decide if I should leave medicine entirely, and try to enter full time ministry. I angrily wrote about how frustrated, and unfair, and impossible this all was. Sometimes I found a glimmer of possibility and dreamed for this book and for you. But then I looked in anguish at several of my friends—suffering under family losses, natural disasters, and horrible illnesses that year. Mostly I wondered if the premise of this entire book was wrong—that sometimes even God couldn't fix things, and life just sucked.

Thankfully, God does not leave us, even in our self-pity and anger.

While I started faithlessly studying for the exam a fourth time, I came across an email from our local Medical Campus Fellowship Outreach that had the title, "When failure is an option." Incredibly enough, it was a talk given by Dr. Tyler Cooper about when he failed an important medical school exam (Step 1) three times, and was dismissed from his medical school. He describes coming to a point where he realized he was at a crossroads and had to make the decision to choose God's life for himself, or to stay on his own course. He decided to trust God, whether that ended with him finishing medical school or not.

It's wonderful when God answers out prayers the way we expect and life goes according to plans. But it's much more difficult to continue to trust God when it doesn't. Dr. Cooper said he had to come to a place where he realized that the test/that decision/that outcome did not define who he was. Passing the test was not what ultimately mattered. God was using that particular difficulty to draw him closer. He had to get to a point where he was willing to trust God, no matter what the end turned out to be.

When he came to that realization, incredibly enough, Dr. Cooper's medical school called, explaining that they had re-written the requirements. He was allowed to take the test a fourth time, if he appealed. Thankfully, that time he passed. Not because he studied harder. Not because God always blesses those who follow Him. But because God had a plan for him and knew exactly how to get *both his life and heart positioned where God needed him*, in order to be able to use him best.

Thankfully, God reminds us that even if we don't get our prayers answered in exactly the way we want, He still has the power to redeem and renew and rewrite those things that are our fault, others' sins, and part of a cursed world. However low we may get, He's neither afraid of, surprised by, or frustrated by the things that terrify us. And He, unlike the things around us, will never change, never fail, and never give up on us, no matter how hopeless it looks.

Struggle and Disappointment

"Well, it looks like you just submitted it late—you were supposed to submit it on the 29th."

I clenched the phone with a death grip and clamped my jaw shut not to yell through the phone. I was looking at the email that said I was supposed to submit my work hours on the 31st. I had specifically called the week before and asked if

I could get paid any sooner. I had been told no, the best I could do was wait until the 7th to get paid. It was the 8th. I was still broke. And now I was just plain angry.

The voice on the other end went on to keep talking about how usually it was due the 31st, but this particular hospital paid biweekly, not bimonthly, which was a little different, and I would get paid in two more weeks, if I just waited. I put down the phone as she kept rambling, and stared incredulously at it. I just couldn't win.

My head started swimming with memories of the last few months. My budget had been made made assuming that I wouldn't work for two months, but I hadn't had a steady job in five months. Of course financial issues arose. First, this job fell through, then that one. The one that should have been perfect, the one that would have sucked but was still a job....

I spent many years holding my bleeding heart, waiting for it to be healed, waiting for life to calm down and be normal. But it never did. I was waiting for the Hallmark movie ending where all the pain equaled a great new opportunity. But the more things crumbled around me, the more bitter and hopeless I got—what was the point of dreaming or trying, if you just ended up getting punished for it in the end? I couldn't get out of the "world is falling apart" mindset.

Life had become a place of struggle and heartache, and I often just hated it all. I was three years out of finishing my residency, and I had somehow become a doctor who couldn't pass a test or find a job. Then I ended up in the middle of nowhere in a temp job with no friends, no prospects, no money, and what felt like no shot at changing anything. I had dreamed for years of traveling and teaching—and I couldn't even afford to pay for the gas in the rental car they loaned me.

Sitting there with all my broken dreams, and outlandish problems, I kept thinking back to a journal entry from when I was in college. It had rambled on about how I wanted to change the world. And back then, when I was "just a child," before I had seen so much pain, death, and hatred, anything really did seem possible. But where does hope come from if all you have is the real world, tearing you down no matter where you turn, or what you do?

You stop looking at the pain. And you look up.

When I started writing this book I figured I was onto something—not only for you, but also for my own healing. We have hope as Christians, because of what Jesus did on the cross, not because of what we see in front of us on a particular day. And it's because of Jesus' faithful love that we are able to believe for more today and in the future. It's because of Him that we have hope for anything at all. And you only keep that perspective by focusing on Someone that doesn't ever change—and that's God.

You don't become a great leader by being perfect. You don't become a great leader by getting everything exactly right. You don't become a great leader by always having good news.

You become a great leader by having a vision that gets you through the devastation.

155

By having a foundation that doesn't crack when everything else does. By trusting in God even when all you see is storms. By believing that even when you're discouraged and broken, and at the end of your rope—God will not let you go. *And I promise you, no matter what you do, He will never let you go.*

The way I ended up making it through was not a single, awe-inspiring event. I didn't go to an amazing conference or meet a person with all the answers. I didn't walk into church one day and get a clear revelation that the hopelessness would go away. Trepidation and confusion continued through the next year, as I anxiously studied for boards a fourth time, and—incredibly enough—*finally passed.*

Because I had had a clear word from God that I would be a doctor unlike anything I'd seen before—even if my circumstances refused to agree with God's word over my life— I was going to keep putting one foot in front of the other. Even if I didn't even believe the vision I was working toward, I would commit to try the simplest thing I could think of every day. I used whatever faith was left to try to believe and continue to fight, until my circumstances, and God's plans aligned once again.

You will have setbacks in your career. Some setbacks you'll overcome with no effort. Others will expose weaknesses, or past hurts that can paralyze you. But even if they change your life—you can't let those problems disqualify you. You have to hold on to your identity in Christ, the foundations you have laid in the past, and the vision He's given you for your work (even if it is not completely clear yet). God uses the least likely people in the Bible because they're broken enough to hold a death-grip onto Him—instead of clinging to their failures, setbacks, and their fears. Anyone who can manage to keep trusting God in spite of them, is a true winner in His book.

Further Questions for review:

1) Have you suffered any big setbacks or failures in your career, or know anyone who has?
   How were they dealt with?

2) What is most encouraging about your faith, when you are faced with a disappointment?

3) Has God given you a vision for your career?
   Will you spend some time praying and believing for direction now?

Further Study: To think more about this topic, take a look through the recommendations and stories in John Maxwell's book, *Failing Forward.*

Why Work?

*"You may choose to look the other way but you can never again
say that you did not know."* ~William Wilburforce

*"True godliness does not turn men out of the world,
but enables them to live better in it
and excites their endeavors to mend it."*
~William Penn

*"There is always the danger that we may do the work for
the sake of the work. This is where the respect and love and the
devotion come in—that we do it to God, to Christ,
and that's why we try to do it as beautifully as possible."*
~Mother Teresa

One thing that has changed over the years is the way
we view work. Not long ago, I read an essay by Dorothy Sayers.
She wrote of how, over time, people had changed their view of
the work day and expectations surrounding it. Today, work is
often viewed as required drudgery that must be endured.
Some seem to work mindlessly through 300 days, with the
aim of getting two weeks of vacation. Or retirement. Or some
sabbatical, or another dream that involves leaving the
workforce all together. But work was not always been viewed
as a negative to be suffered through. It wasn't even viewed as

a way to make lots of extra money, so that the sacrifices we had made by working those extra hours could be rewarded by the ability to purchase more upgrades.

Sayers' essay says, "there are only two real sources of wealth—the fruit of the earth and the labor of men." Is that normally how we view the things we study, and the things we create each day? As true wealth? What if the end goal of our work was not to be compensated, but a process to be enjoyed?

Not all of the workplace is beautiful, and obviously not all of it is enjoyable—but is it really as bad as we sometimes make it out to be? Is the problem really the job, or is it more the way we view it? What if the goal wasn't the grade, or the promotion, or the contract, or the satisfied customer—what if the goal was finding pleasure, satisfaction, and enjoyment in the process of the work?

God never promised that we would enjoy everything that we do here on earth. But as children of God couldn't we find better fulfillment in our lives than a two-week vacation? As anointed, appointed heirs, could we provide more answers for the meaning of work to the rest of our colleagues? As leaders of the marketplace, could we enjoy and appreciate the sacrifices we have made for our careers as jewels on a journey, instead of pebbles in our shoes?

I spent too much time during my training, frustrated, waiting for the future, when I assumed it would pay off. But the truth is, we don't need earlier retirement, more travel expenses, or better pay for a worthwhile life. As simple as it sounds, we just need to better appreciate what we have at that time. Our goal should not be to get away from work—but to value and enjoy it.

Maybe my eleven years of training wouldn't have seemed so long if I had stopped resenting all the Saturday nights I spent studying, and instead thanked God for a position that allowed me to do what I do best for years on end—learn. I love to learn! *It's a new instrument, I want to try! This dance move looks fun, show me how it goes! Yes, I read her first book, I really want to read the rest!* If only I had thought of medical school like that, instead of as a painful knife in my back!

Did I really suffer as badly as I complained? Or did I just miss a myriad of opportunities to learn, grow, change, renew, and enjoy things? Maybe it wasn't "the man" or "the system" out to "get me" at all. Maybe God used these life-lessons to mold and make me into who I am today.

Our mission for God means that our work can be worship and has great value to God. So, then our joy comes from doing our work well, instead of avoiding it well. "If your heart is not wholly in the work, the work will not be good—and work that is not good serves neither God nor the community." But if we treat our work like a positive journey that glorifies God, it changes things.

John 14:12 says "...whoever believes in me will also do the works that I do; and greater works than these will he do..." Jesus was saying that the same miracle working, wisely spoken, excellently handled, incredibly miraculous things that He did would explode into incredible new opportunities for us, with the power of the Holy Spirit. So maybe that challenge at your workplace is the renewal that God wants you to jump on top of, instead of letting it overwhelm you. This book exists because I was tired of not being able to find books targeting graduate students and young professionals! It was a thorn in my side that I finally decided to stop complaining about, and instead to write—hopefully to make it easier for you.

I realize in general I am not great at seeing things in a positive light—I am great at complaining! On the last mission trip I took to Colombia, we were awakened the first morning by a frenzied phone call about one of the team members who was feeling sick. The leader handed me the phone as I began quickly pulling on pants, finding a breath mint and a hat, and running out the door. We had a large team, so we were spread out at two hotels, and of course the person who was sick was at the other hotel—two blocks away. The caller had described how the team member was having chest pain and trouble breathing. He had sickle cell disease, and at our high elevation, might be struggling for oxygen, and there might be complications. Should he just grab a cab and head to the nearest hospital...?

My head was spinning with facts as I tried to grab things, direct people, and run to the other hotel. *I need the pulse oximeter the nurse brought, and then someone to walk with me down the sketchy street... No, you can't take a cab to the nearest hospital— that's an hour away and if he's not stable that's not wise... I need more cash—not American dollars—where did I put the money we had already exchanged?... Which is the closest medical center that might be open at 6 a.m. and who was going to go...?*

All kinds of scenarios were running through my head as my heart was thumping... *Crazy doctor takes too long running down the street and team member just trying to do good ends up suffocating...* My thoughts were scattered, but mostly I was all the while grumbling that I wasn't supposed to wake up at the crack of dawn and run to an ailing patient anymore—I was no longer a resident—I worked in a calm, collected clinic at normal hours and hated starting my days in a worried frenzy like this!

But in the midst of my whirring mind, there was one thought that wouldn't go away. It was the thought that this was not a medical problem, but a spiritual one. No matter how many times I tried to shake it out and refocus—it just kept coming back. I started praying and tried to explain to God that this was a ridiculous thought...

"God, I am a doctor. I can't tell a person with a diagnosed medical disease that we are not taking them to the hospital and instead we are going to pray for them!"

And the reply from the Holy Spirit? *Why not?*

So, we prayed. And he didn't need to go to the hospital.

When God gets involved, it isn't bread and butter medicine anymore—it's bigger than just what I know and what I bring. It's bigger than my own fears. It's bigger than my own doubts. It's bigger than my own complaints. It's God moving the boundaries of my paradigm of medical realities and "the way it's always been done." It's God who rewrites the way, the reason, and the power with which we work every single day.

Will you dare to believe that could be true for your workplace, too? *Why not?*

Every idea and action does not have to be something world-changing, it may just be small. For my patients who are struggling with weight loss, I frequently concentrate on what they are drinking. The average soda contains a lot of sugar (39 grams), and the average juice box as well (23 grams); so consuming one glass of juice or soda a day for a year is equivalent to 35 lbs. of sugar, or 15 lbs. of weight gained. Cut that drink out, and it becomes a super small change with a whole lot of impact.

In our workplace, what if we could each find our niche and make an impact on it? What if we stopped pretending Jesus only existed inside church walls and let Him into our lives every day? What if we could impact the number of medical students, and lawyers, and graduate students who tried to kill themselves—overwhelmed by their own self-pressure—unable to make sense of the life they have chosen? What if we called people to another level of excellence at their work? What if people were daily encouraged and challenged to grow both creatively, practically, and spiritually at their place of work? What if people were able to re-write their careers and their place of work with the gifts that God had given them? What if we fought for more than a few extra cents an hour or more vacation time? What if we were fighting for people's lives, people's possibilities, people's cultures? What if God could re-write the things we thought were impossible or unexpected or unreachable dreams, and get us back to believing in the miraculous? What if we each had written on our hearts that God had called us to change the world? Could we live our lives like that? *Why not?*

Further Questions for review:

1) How do you generally feel about the work you do each day? Positive or negative? Dedicated or trying to leave?

2) Do you see your position at your work as an opportunity to change and redeem things around you?

3) If that was the goal and the vision you had in your heart—what would that kind of work day look like for you?

4) Before you go on, spend some time thinking and praying about the small little changes in your views of work, and your way of living out your work day, that over time, could make a huge impact in your world.

Changing Our Priorities

How to Change the World

"Often what we need is not more data but more insight into the data we already have."
~Wayne Grudem

"You can find God in the laboratory, just as much as in the cathedral."
~Francis Collins

If you've been thinking, *"Okay, Ashley, you've said a lot of stuff here, but you have kind of been rambling. I need you to get more specific. I do want to make a difference in the world. How exactly do I go about it?"* Have no fear, we are finally to that section! Here is what you need to do: simply trust God.

One thing I've seen a lot recently is we have to be very careful how we define, "changing the world" and "finding a meaningful career." To reiterate —**what we do cannot define our value**. How many millions we make, whether or not our company feeds the homeless, and whether we believe our actions are inherently good doesn't make our work meaningful. If the value of the work you do hangs on external markers, it will always be fleeting. The signature of your work only comes from God. Everything else gets added onto that. Then you have significance, whether your everyday work is cleaning a fork, or literally changing the world.

In this book, we have covered topics of discipleship, evangelism, and leadership. Which of these speak to you the most? Pray about it and focus on deepening your thinking in that category. Make one of them a priority in your life, in your vocation, right now—knowing that the others will find their place. The one you choose will set you apart from everyone else. One of them is a God-given gift, that you should nurture at your place of work.

I have made *discipleship* my priority for most of my career—and the opportunity to practice it comes up all the time. I'll talk to coworkers over lunch breaks about their God-given design; I'll be connected with students that need a little direction in their profession; or I'll take the time to encourage or teach others how God has gotten me where I am. Mostly, discipleship has involved me picking out one person a year— someone I met at church, a student, a coworker—and just keeping them at the forefront of my mind. Praying for them. Texting and emailing them encouragement. Inviting them to do anything I'm doing— come to this birthday party, come to the gym, come to church with me. It's not hard if I just make it a priority to keep them around me, and say what God brings to my mind when we are together.

Don't forget—the focus of your career isn't going to be stewarding the lives of other Christians, or even to get people saved, as much as it is to do the work He has called you to do.

You have a career, and that is your priority. As the representative of God, you are going to have access to places your pastor would never go—in your field, in your relationships, and in your ideas. Go, working excellently with your skills, and with the vision to look for opportunities God will inevitably give you to disciple, evangelize, and lead those around you. Go looking for that challenge, but don't go neglecting the work God initially called you to do.

Some of you may be saying, "One more thing you missed, Ashley. I don't know what I am called to do for work!! Where do I go from here?" God's primary personal goal for each one of us is to know Christ and to become more like Him.

First, have you honestly asked God what *He has in mind for you* and your career? And then—have *you listened and waited for the answers*? Sometimes the answers don't come in a direct answer, or in the way we expect. The reason I went across the country for college is not because I heard a booming, "Go to school there, Ashley" from heaven. I got scholarships to go there! And the same for medical school. For a poor student without a lot of savings, that is a lights blinking, miraculous sign! Sometimes God arranges things in a certain way to move us toward our goals, whether we realize it at the time, or can only see it in hindsight.

But when it came down to choosing a residency program or a job after graduation, I had more options. I made lists, went through pros and cons, prayed for a clear answer as to which location—and came up with nothing clear. So, I just picked! Oh no! *Does that mean it's not of God because it was my choice?*

A pastor of mine taught me that God gives us choices and we cannot sit, unmoving, afraid, waiting for Him to tell us everything. You know this on some level—you didn't sit in prayer for hours this morning before you decided what to wear, eat for breakfast, or which way to drive to work. Even if you did pray about those things, you eventually made a choice! In the garden of Eden, God instructed Adam to choose the names of the animals. Do you think Adam needed a special, personal word from God for every single creature he named? God gave him the task, and the freedom to make the decisions as well.

Sometimes God will give personal direction very clearly. Other times we have to choose, and watch as He redirects, and nudges us in the directions He has in mind for us. If we have our foundations set, and are listening for His direction, we will begin to notice the subtle ways God is both leading, and letting us choose. And if we do start walking in the wrong direction, I promise, He will re-direct.

Either way, God doesn't leave you alone to fend for yourself. Whether you've got an established 20-year plan or an unsettled 1-week strategy, He is still there. He is not only your Father and your friend, He is still in charge. And your Boss is awesome. Trust Him to lead you on the life-long road, where He is calling you...it is not a one-stop destination.

The world we live in is not a movie—you are not the supporting actor for another great lead actor's life. Everyone's path will not look the same, but your own significant path will be given by God in the right time. And as you go, you will see how your gifts interact with those around you.

Here's a wonderful reminder, especially if you're still not sure yet about your direction...

Who am I?

If God is my Father, then I am His child.

I am not just an ant trying to eke out an existence on this planet. I am significant. In fact, I have been born into a kingly and priestly family. I can rule over the affairs of life. I have access to God. If I have a covenant with God, then I have the Most Supreme Partner. He is wise and wealthy. If I work with Him, then I am bound to be successful. If God—the Creator of the Universe—is working with me and I am created in His image, then I can be creative. With His breath in me, I will have His thoughts and His perspective. I will have energy to rise above the problems of life. I will have innovative ideas that haven't yet occurred to anyone else. I will ask Him, and He may give to me ways to expand His kingdom into business, government, and every area of society in which He desires to express Himself and establish rulership. If I am created in God's image, then I have a mind that can conceive, a heart that can dream, and a spirit that can soar. If God is with me, the limits are off and the future is open.

Further Questions for review:

1) Do you have definite career plans or are you still working it out?
   How have you seen God's leading in your vocational choices so far?

2) Do you resonate with a desire to find work that meaningfully impacts the world we live in?
   How have your thoughts on that changed throughout reading this book?

3) Which of these three—discipleship, evangelism, or leadership—will be your main priority for work going forward?
   What might that look like for you?

Teamwork and Legacy

*"The battle for truth in our relationships is often fought
in our own heads and hearts."*
~Melissa Spoelstra

*"Here you leave today and enter the world of
yesterday, tomorrow, and fantasy."*
~Walt Disney

*"You are positioned to shed life, light, and hope
everywhere you go."*
~Rene Rochester

In medical school, we were required to do research for a summer. I signed up to go with a local doctor on a week-long mission trip to Sierra Leone, West Africa to teach leadership skills. Then I would stay for another five weeks and do research for my paper. My thesis was to survey local people and determine what other things the local clinic could provide. It sounded straight-forward, but I didn't realize how complicated it would be.

Sierra Leone was a country ripped apart by a civil war that had demoted them from being one of the premier countries in Africa to the second poorest country in the world. Anyone with any education or shred of money had fled the country in the previous decades, so things were pretty chaotic. There were bathrooms, but no running water, because pipes had been sold for money. There were cars, but roads were

171

barely drivable. There were light bulbs, but we only had 10 hours of electricity that whole summer.

I was supposed to create a paper from the work I did, but that proved impossible. Most people I interviewed were not educated and had no opinions on their health. The most common answer was, "They treat me fine," with no desire for any improvements. Also, they had barely had health care during the past 30 years, so had a totally different concept of health. When I would ask, "When is the last time you were sick?" to a fifty-year-old man, he would reply, "I've never been sick." My surveys did not reflect reality.

Being in Sierra Leone impacted me personally. I redefined "excellent care," "predictors of health," and "public health needs" in a huge way. And after having spent years in college, terrified of going abroad, it became my new goal in life. When I graduated from residency, I worked for a while planning medical mission trips. But after a few years, finances made that impossible, and I passed the trip-planning on to someone else.

As I sat around dejected, depressed, and burned out, friends suggested many options—but none would create a legitimate career that combined medicine, missions, and a paycheck. The most common suggestion was that I create my own "mission agency" to do trips by myself. My answer was always no—that stemmed from my time in Sierra Leone.

As I spent time shadowing at several medical locations in Sierra Leone, one of my favorites was an eye clinic. It had been supported by a nonprofit for over a decade. Initially, there was a team of American eye doctors that worked full time. Then, they spent years paying for local people to go to a university for eye school training (outside of Sierra Leone since all of the universities were closed). They then returned to take over patient care. As the clinic became self-sufficient, they discovered they were receiving counterfeit medications. So, they created a new plan—send others to school to learn how to synthesize medications—and buy a new set of equipment to do it in the clinic. By the time I arrived, it was totally directed by Sierra Leone natives, and was the only one of its kind in the country. I was inspired by this small organization and all they had accomplished—with a lot of planning and time.

The main thing I learned from this organization was the power of a team.

I spent most of the summer as the only American dreaming, wishing, and lamenting the limitations I encountered. I was able to teach some nurses how to make a spreadsheet of patient information, but there were many more steps needed to get them to be functional and self-sufficient. I realized one main strength of the eye clinic was they didn't put all of the knowledge, and training, and strengths on a single person—they put everything into a team built to last. I promised myself that the next time I went abroad, I wouldn't go alone, I would go with a team. And I would go with a plan to build something that would be bigger than a single research paper, and that was made to outlast me—to become a legacy.

Missions has taught me that teamwork adds gifts to me that I wouldn't otherwise have. You put quiet little me in a sea of hundreds of patients, where I don't speak the language, and I'm largely useless. But if you add in organization, a translator, a loud leader, and an evangelist—it ramps my own personal influence. God doesn't need a hundred of me running around—God needs me paired with someone who is better at gathering crowds, paired with someone who is great at business, paired with someone who has the next great idea for social justice. None of those gifts are mine, and although I can learn about them, that is still not as good as pairing me with someone who excels at them. *Teamwork makes the dream work,* because it really does give you abilities you wouldn't have had alone.

Don't misunderstand me—sometimes you do have to build and imagine and work alone. Sometimes you are a catalyst that gets everyone else positioned to go—and worry about recruiting later! There is value in going alone, but if I can take someone else with me and create a culture of change, it's a much bigger punch.

On a mission trip to Bolivia years ago, we had a leadership conference on a college campus. We spent all day inviting people, me contributing with my broken Spanish and lame dance moves to get people's attention. After the program was over, I talked with one of the young students and asked how he had heard about the conference.

He replied, "I was dragged in here."

I figured I must be misunderstanding him, so I asked again, "What do you mean? Did a friend make you come?"

He replied, "No, I was outside, and this guy grabbed my arm, pulled on it, and dragged me toward him until I followed him inside." The student wasn't bothered by it at all, and thanked us for the great lessons of the conference.

But I begged him to explain more. "What happened? What guy?"

He looked around and pointed out one of the men on our mission team—a bald, ex-military guy with a limp in his thirties, who I knew didn't speak any Spanish. I apologized to the student and walked over to confront the team member, who I feared might have taken the instruction to "invite people to the conference" a bit too far!

When I confronted him, he wasn't even apologetic. "Look, I can't participate in the dances, I can't give medical care like you, and I can't even speak Spanish. I ran out of flyers. I refused to make excuses anymore about what I couldn't do. All I've got is my arms and a smile on my face— but I got a dozen guys to come in tonight, with just what I had. **What more did God ask of me than to do my best with what I was given**?" I couldn't have agreed more.

Building a legacy does not mean looking for people who are just like you, but for people with gifts that complete yours, who can walk with you in fulfilling both your dreams and theirs. Legacy is planning to leave something behind, besides just the physical work. It's leaving behind the sparks of dreams and goals you had in someone else, who will keep the fires going even when you are gone.

Sometimes legacy is planting something solid that outlasts you. When I traveled to Peru I was struck by the unique architecture. Many of the buildings had a dark reddish brown, brick pattern on the lower two feet of the building, but the rest of the wall was a smooth white material with modern architectural decor. It wasn't until we made friends with a local Peruvian history buff that I understood why. The Incas—who also built the famous Machu Picchu—had constructed the buildings of dark reddish brown brick hundreds of years ago. When the Spanish took over the country, they realized how strong the foundations were. Instead of demolishing them, they built their new walls on top of the old. I don't know if there are any architects out there—but I'm told this is quite an incredible feat, since foundations are hard to lay, are designed based on weight, and do not usually last hundreds of years! But those who had the knowledge and desire built a legacy that outlasted themselves, their children, and even their children's children. Those of us who have that same mindset can leave a legacy by building "structures" that will stand long after we're gone. Does your field tend to build like this? Are you laying down foundations that will not only stay strong after you're gone, but will also be able to support other new dreams and goals as well?

Even when you don't have a literal team you are working with, you have a group of people that contribute to you and thus to your work. We've talked about the Mission of God and how He left to the church the task of changing our lives, others' lives, and the culture around us. He gave us the mission of loving one another. That can be hard, even in

Christian relationships. But Christ said that the world would know that we are Christians by the way we love one another.

You have to keep this in mind when you are building a team and it feels like it is more trouble than it's worth. However, you cannot enter into the work God has for you, until you can enter into the relationships he has for you. Relationships that stretch you will make you grow in your personal life, and in your vision—personally and corporately. He's got a team to walk with you, as you go.

My personal team that walks with me is often not in my current field. The people that encourage my faith the most are my friends in campus ministry. The friends that improve my scientific mindset the most don't believe in the traditional health care system at all. My friends who work as teachers taught me to value the process of communication involved in learning. It is this wonderful combination of influencers that have made me better than I could have become on my own.

My team hasn't always looked the way I wanted it to. My team has consisted of people who actually treated me quite poorly—but showed me who I didn't want to become. My team has consisted of people who got on my nerves, but taught me patience I wouldn't have known otherwise! My team has consisted of people of different ages and different stages, that I should have had nothing in common with; but somehow, they awakened a drive for something I never knew I wanted to pursue. Have I mentioned that I played in a bluegrass band when I was in medical school? I promise you—that was not remotely on my list of things to do! But it honestly shaped me into who I am today (and oddly enough, gave me something fun to talk about on all my interviews!)

But more than anything, my team is bigger than just me and my books. Most of us in the academic world value mentors and references, and maybe even people to laugh with on the weekends. But how much do we value those who are going to pull us out of the habits we get stuck in, or who can call us to another level of greatness?

Who is on your team? Who is stretching you and encouraging you to come out of the box you made for your career? How are you doing gathering a team to fight with, and finding a legacy to pour into?

Further Questions for review:

1) Do you have people around you that teach you things you wouldn't have learned otherwise?

2) Who is in your life that you would normally avoid, but that God put there to make you better?

3) Does your field ever talk about legacy?
   What does/could that look like?

The Beauty of the Mundane

*"Failure looks like a gray place where we couldn't tell
when we were at work and when we weren't."*
~Raechel Myers

*"To whom he said, 'This is the resting place, let the weary rest,'
and 'this is the place of repose'- but they would not listen. So then,
the Word of the Lord will become to them: "Do this, do that, a
rule for this, a rule for that; a little here, a little there- so that as
they go they will fall backward; they will be injured and snared
and captured."*
~Isaiah 28:12-13 (NIV)

The first medical mission trip that I helped plan was to Bolivia, where we two doctors saw over 700 patients. We gave out free medications, social work help, and prayed with many people who gave their lives to Christ. I saw the pastor months later and he told us they had so many new church members that the building was overflowing, and they needed time to get organized before they could have us come back. It was an incredible trip with many amazing wins.

Although I start with that story, this chapter is to remind you of one thing—most days of your life will not be an incredible testimony like this. Many people live their lives waiting for the highs—the incredible destination vacation, the next life-changing conference, the greatest new fad, or most remarkable new experience. But it's taken me a long time to realize that life isn't worth living if most of it is sitting around waiting for the next great thing. What about all the things you miss in between, while you wait for something huge and spectacular?

When was the last time you were overjoyed doing your least favorite part of your job? When was the last time you spent marveling at all the incredible things that had to happen in your mind for you to read this sentence? When was the last time you sat and enjoyed the boring, rather than sat anxiously waiting for something remarkable? Remember Brother Lawrence who made *every* action of his life an act of worship to God?

The beauty of the mundane is hard for a storyteller and a perfectionist like me. When it's all said and done, boring doesn't sell! It's hard to make a viral post, or a marketing tactic, or a memorable story out of it. Usually, regular days completely fade away with time. In the meantime, it's too easy to get distracted by all the things we dislike, or all the things that don't work, instead of noticing all of the numerous, tiny, beautiful things that do.

When I first started planning medical trips, the first three-to-six months were pretty awkward—I didn't have a clue what to do with my time. I'd spend hours researching Bolivia—politics, hospitals available, medication costs, vaccination rates, social justice work being done there—whatever I could think up that might relate to our trip.

But after all that research, there would be six hours left in the work day!! Do you know what I ended up doing many days? Folding t-shirts. And in case that wasn't clear—I literally mean I would fold t-shirts! We had several hundred people sign up for mission trips, and every person would get at least two t-shirts. So, I spent many hours folding and organizing hundreds of shirts. I was told by the rest of the team I was "good at it." To clarify, I do not have a degree in folding shirts! I simply like things to be neat. Don't get me wrong, I complained in my head, *I went to medical school, and I am a doctor, and you want me to fold shirts? Seriously?*" But, I choked back my pride and got back to work.

It may sound crazy, but I came to love folding shirts. I made the choice not to just sit there and fold. I would pray for the person going on the trip and believe God for an incredible opportunity for them and for that country. I would imagine that the neat arrangement would bless the person who opened the box. Also, after having spent years in a hospital, I would thank God for the beauty of a simple day, where I only had to fold t-shirts, and didn't have to watch any children suffer or die of their illness. It was mundane, and seemingly endless, and quite boring at times. But ultimately, it wasn't just about a shirt to me—I honestly came to the point of experiencing joy that was hidden in performing that simple little task.

Now obviously, I don't always appreciate the mundane. Folding t-shirts seemed totally unrelated when I was actually in Bolivia. The second day of medical clinics, I saw 122 patients, which is six times my normal. Many were complaining of simple pains, and we gave them an over-the-counter pain killer—very straightforward medically. I was physically exhausted at trying to literally wrap myself around screaming children to get a better glimpse in their ears. I was mentally exhausted at running down lists of symptoms, differentials, and medications. I was emotionally exhausted at the heartache and lack of amenities available. And I was spiritually exhausted—having prayed for so many needs. And mostly, I was just a little heartbroken. I had prayed and believed God that I would see healing on this trip—a true, miracle-level testimony of actual physical healing. But there I was without *one*, when the medical outreach was over.

I wish I could say the next thing I thought was, *"That was not life-changing, but it was beautiful. I did what God asked of me, and what more was there to do?"* But I definitely didn't. I sat overwhelmed and upset about my bad headache. Because it's easy to complain and only concentrate on all the things that didn't go perfectly—but it's much harder to remember in the hard, and the boring, and the painful moments—that God is still in control.

On Friday morning, we had a change in schedule and were able to go set up another clinic. It was a great day because it was just a tad slower and we had more time with patients. But it was also great, because I had stopped worrying about collecting miracles before my eyes, and I had just asked God to use me. Not surprisingly, when I took the pressure off, that's when the miracles started.

My favorite memory was heartbreaking when I first saw him—a gentleman in his fifties with graying hair, about six-feet tall and about 120 lbs., slowly limped in and sat down. I was immediately afraid. Kids are my specialty, but when I am abroad I sometimes see adults to help out. This particular man did not look well at all—this was not going to be a simple headache. He had been having bad mid-abdominal pain, vomiting, and fevers for the past several months, and lost tons of weight. I really got nervous. I may not see adults all the time, but I remembered this example from medical school—it was classic for pancreatic cancer. Most people have two months to live from the time of diagnosis. I knew he needed several body scans we could not do, several specialists we did not have, and medications we hadn't brought. We didn't even have an anti-nausea medication with us! I literally had nothing to offer this man, except a likely diagnosis of his coming death.

Whenever I get to the edge of my own knowledge, I start praying. And I simply asked God what else I could do. God replied to me that this was an attack on his life because he would not forgive someone. I blinked in confusion—I was trying to ask God what medicine I should use—the reply was not what I was expecting at all! But I asked the patient if he believed in God, and he said he did. I told him what God said, and asked him if he needed to forgive someone. He and the interpreter discussed it for a while. I asked him if he would say out loud that he forgave the person. He replied no. Now I was really stuck. I couldn't make him forgive the person, but the entire meeting was hinging on that. After a brief silence, he spoke up again saying that he needed to go apologize to his friend in person right now. And in that moment, the entire atmosphere of the room changed. The Bible says that where two or more are gathered in his name, God is with them. We could literally feel God's presence with us. There was a loving, and also awe-inspiring change in the room that refused to let this man suffer any more and changed his entire life. Together we prayed for a healing from illness, protection for his life, and

God's blessing in everything. Incredibly enough, he was completely healed.

I share this story because it is an incredible memory, and a reminder of what God can do. *But, I had spent almost ten years praying and waiting for a miracle like that.* I remember talking with a nursing student on another mission trip. I called her "my shadow." She was in tears as I tried to encourage her with the truth: even without miracles, our simple daily tasks convey God's presence, and bless those we minister to.

I can't spend my life waiting for more miraculous moments before I trust God, or pray for someone, or step out in faith. Most days do not include incredible things like a man being healed of cancer. Most days when I go into a clinical setting, it is very predictable. Most days when I try to ask people if they want to accept Jesus as their Savior, the answer is no. Most days are not incredible stories of God giving me exactly what I ask for, in the way that I expect it. Most days are very mundane, very quiet, and very regular. Most days are me somewhere in the background, doing something quiet, and unnoticeable, and unimportant like folding shirts! But it's staying faithful, and joyful, and expectant in those boring days that make me ready to go when the incredible days come around. We can't live our lives only giving credit and appreciation to the miraculous days—because then we completely discredit all the other tiny miracles God is giving us with every single breath.

This does not mean we can't ask for those incredible days and miracles. It simply means we can't build our lives on them. Following God is not worth it, *if* we're doing it to see miracles. Following God is worth it, *and* I get to see miracles. It's a tiny distinction that makes all the difference in how we view God, and our lives. God expects us to live our lives filled with faith. God is a miracle-working God, so we shouldn't sell Him short and settle only for the things we see here and now. He expects us to believe for more. But we believe not because they give our lives meaning and credibility, but because they glorify His Name.

Resting in God

The second painful mundane thing to remember as you build—***you must rest.*** Someone just moaned at that last statement and deemed me crazy. Was I even paying attention to all the things I just said? *"Minister here, serve here, excel here... obviously rest is not an option!! Ashley, I have places to go, goals to reach, and things to do—and your ridiculous thoughts of 'enjoying the mundane' and 'taking time to rest' are completely absurd!"*

I know they are. Because I know the world you live in! I know what it's like to study every waking hour of every day, and still fail the test. I know what it's like to try to connect with peers, impress bosses, and find time to notice anyone and anything else. I know what it's like to have extra projects beyond regular assignments looming over your head, to give you the extra points on your resume, so you will stand out and get where you're trying to go. I know what it's like to give up everything for your work—your sleep, your meals, your bathroom breaks, your plans, your friends, your weekends, your vacation time, your holidays—to do what has to be done—so one day you can get where you need to be! I know what it's like to run the race. ***But even more than that, I know what it's like to burn out because of it.***

I'm in my early thirties. But I know what it's like to burn out of your career—I've already done it twice. I know what it's like to put so much pressure on myself, and what I perceive God's expectations to be of me—that I literally run until I can't even see the point of life any more. I know what it's like to see all my hard work go up in flames. And I know what it's like to come to the crushing reality that most of what wore me out was not the job, or the school, or the expectations—but my own inability to value rest.

God didn't create us to run like we force ourselves to do. There are special projects that require much to be completed with excellence. But far too often, we let them take over our lives. We let the race and the stress become our only option. That was never God's plan. And although it's terrifying, we have to take time to rest—and trust God truly to take care of everything else.

For instance, I like to sum up Abraham's life in two simple sentences: He moved where God told him. And then he waited for what God promised him. That was his whole story in the Bible! Even non-Christians know his name now, because his sole goal was to trust God no matter what, and he did. He waited for God's promises, and then for God's timing, and when he did, he left a legacy greater than the stars in the sky or the grains of sand along the beach *(Genesis 22:17)*.

We have to grasp the importance of resting and waiting in our own lives. I did fairly well through medical school— I took my own personal sabbath by spending an evening a week with God, becoming rejuvenated, so that I could be at my best. After that it got really messy. I know it's crucial, and I teach about it all the time. It's easy to say—and another thing entirely to live. But it does work! God gives simple blessings in the most stressed parts of life, when you take the time to put Him first. It's the gift of a random afternoon off, so you can catch up—since you spent the night before taking time to rest with God. It's an assignment being pushed back literally two weeks, so you actually have time to make it. It's possible.

Residency was a long struggle for me because of the illness I had suffered. I spent many nights crying for hours and begging God to change things. Later, God actually told me that those were His favorite nights. Those nights were my nightmares—I didn't like feeling weak and admitting that I was scared or overworked! *But God said those were His favorites, because it was me spending time being honest with Him.*

Taking a sabbath doesn't have to be a happy thing. If you need to spend an hour yelling at God about how bad your week was, then do it—if it's real! But take the time to get out of the "work bubble," and get back to you and God. That little bit of set-aside time is where God meets you. It's where your life gets refocused on what matters. It's where you get re-energized to get back in.

Back to the struggle. Back to the painful. Back to prayers that seemingly are not answered. And one day—back to the incredible testimonies, and dreams, and beauty that await for those who waded through the mundane.

Further Questions for Review:

1) What is the most taxing part of your life right now? Is there another way to look at that task or requirement from God's perspective, that might make it less painful?

2) Are you more likely to drown in the mundane or ignore it? Are you keeping a healthy but expectant posture toward miracles in your life?

3) How are you doing prioritizing a sabbath in your life? What does look like for you?
   What could make that time more meaningful for you and God

Independence vs. Love

*"The meaning of life came to be seen as the fruit of the freedom
of the individual to choose the life that most fulfills him or her
personally... Our culture makes individual freedom,
autonomy, and fulfillment the very highest values."*
~Timothy Keller

"When love and skill work together, expect a masterpiece."
~John Ruskin

I've got to be honest with you about independence—it
is a hard topic for me to write. I feel like a hypocrite. I could
talk about how important it is to pour into your own spouse
and kids, but I am not married and don't have kids, so maybe
we should leave that topic to someone else. Or, I could discuss
how crucial it is to have a strong connection with your parents,
siblings, and cousins—but I spent my training living 1,200
miles away from them, so clearly, I'm not the best example of
that, either. We could discuss the importance of spiritual
family in your church, but since mine keeps moving away, I
fear I'm not an expert at that either. I've had several projects
where I set out to train someone to take over my position as
leader, but instead, they left entirely. And honestly, part of
why I have so much time to write this book is because I can't
seem to find a job—partially because I am running out of job
references to give future employers—so I'm not even good at

networking. I mentioned knowing your weaknesses is crucial, and I think one of mine is *independence*. So really, I'm just the poster child for what not to do! Maybe that in and of itself will help us discuss this very difficult topic (at least difficult for me).

Where we are going to start and finish this topic is in discussing *love*. I know, I know— somebody just let out a heart-wrenching sigh, somebody decided I was crazy, and somebody probably put the book down and walked away. Let's be real—how many books about marketplace excellence talk about *love* this much? It would be easier if I could lay out a formula of "how to succeed in business" or "how to make it to the top." But I'm not describing how to get you to the top. **I'm discussing all the things that can break you down on your way as you climb.** *And one of the major problems is not understanding love.*

Most of the problems I described above are examples of me not understanding how to love. I know how to work hard. I know how to get the task done, how to solve the problem, and how to make things that are incredible. What I do not do well is love imperfect people. See, I get that *I'm* not perfect. But what I don't always get is the fact that regardless of how much I can do on my own strength, I need other people as well—people who are not perfect. I need people who hate me, people who are just awful humans, people who are selfish, people who are lazy, people who ignore me, and people who walk all over me. I need them all to be able to make it. I may need them to teach me—what to do and what not to do. I may need to oversee them. I may need them to connect me to someone I didn't know. I may need them to break me of something I couldn't see in myself. I may need them to love me in their own broken way. But I can't make it to my dreams on my own. I need them, each and every one. We were not created like one-celled organisms who literally have everything they need within themselves to grow, reproduce, move, and change! We were created to love and to be loved.

Independence is how I was taught to make it in my career, and I suspect for you as well. There were several in my class who tried to make it to the top by backstabbing, putting down, and telling white lies—walking all over me and the rest of our classmates to get there. The world can make it seem like relationships are dispensable, and you don't need anyone but yourself to get where you want to go. But with God, relationship has been the design from the beginning. He has much more in mind than you by yourself—He's got your team!

A good friend was working at a clinic with a boss who was cutting her down daily, questioning everything she did, even when it was right, and constantly arguing. The atmosphere of the workplace was so negative that the employees turned against each other, trying to look good in the eyes of their leader. It dragged on for years.

One day he went to work a completely changed person. He apologized for all the fear and dread he had caused. My friend is now actually discipling him—both in leadership skills and in a relationship with God. And honestly, isn't that just the ending we wanted?! But think about how awful it was for her as an employee in the meantime—trying not to quit. Every week in our Bible study, we prayed—she in tears—as she poured out her frustrations and desire to leave. But because she stayed and fought the only way she knew how—in the prayer closet, she became a much better leader herself. When she becomes a boss, she knows what not to do, she knows the power of words, she knows the power of an apology. And she knows the power of standing strong while working with imperfect lives. It is only in standing through the pain, that you come to see the transformation.

But your story may be more like mine—not ending in the boss doing a 180 turnaround. Maybe it ended with the entire business going under, you having to leave your job, walking away questioning whether or not you had any value, since your boss always referred to you as "replaceable." Maybe you're currently stuck working or living or befriending or discipling someone who is not on the same page as you. Or you're stuck somewhere *in between the lines* of the time you put in, and the great relationships you had expected to follow. If I can encourage you with nothing else—*independence is never the answer.*

Independence seems to be the cry of the generation—we don't really need anyone! We don't need marriages, we don't need relationships, we don't need friends, we don't want labels, we just want to do our own thing—none of these things last anyway, so why fight for them—they're not worth it! The academic world and business worlds, especially, turned from valuing people long ago. The only way to get to the top is to walk over the people around you. The only way to be noticed it to demean your competition. The only way to make it is to leave them all behind. But the Bible says the complete opposite. We're to love the hardest of competitors. We're to turn the other cheek for the evilest of bosses. We're to serve and love on the meanest of classmates and coworkers. And we're to hold on like glue to the people God does bring in our lives—family, friends, enemy, or not. The number one thing you can take to work that your non-Christian coworkers will not even know what to do with—is to simply show love for them.

Professionally and personally I've had many relationships sour in the past few years. A major problem was that I just let them go instead of actually fighting for them. *"This person is clearly not trustworthy, I should probably keep my distance... This person is not honest, I can't trust anything they say... This person clearly doesn't value me, why should I value their opinion?"* Everything I pondered was logical, but it came from my independent mind, and was honestly, unbiblical. There are no verses that say to trust your boss only when your boss is a good person. There are no verses to love your enemy only when you have the energy to do so. There are no verses that Christians should treat others as awfully as they have treated you. Instead, God commands us to love one another. Love not just when we're at church, when telling someone about God, or when circumstances are perfect. Just love, as He loves us.

However, my problem was not just me devaluing relationships—it was a setup! It was a setup to entice me to fall into the same traps the rest of the world is so busy falling in— the trap that our job and our vision is all we need. *But that's a lie from the devil that we cannot afford to believe.* We are designed to be in relationship: "It is not good for man to be alone!" *(Genesis 2:18)* We are created to love and serve one another. And we are equipped to fight and work for our relationships, with the power of God. So instead of cursing, getting mad, getting bitter, and letting my relationships fall apart these last few years—I could have been fighting harder! I could have been praying more against the attacks of the enemy; could have been laying down biblical truth, more than listening to lies; and could have been loving people even when they didn't love me back. Either I will fight for the people God has placed in my life, or I will lose them completely, and be lost—without an army, without a team, without the people that will get me to the goals I value most.

We have to learn to fight for them, no matter what.

The academic and business worlds can never teach you to do that—they don't know or value love. It is something that can only come from God. And more godly love is what your place of work or study needs most. Love at your office isn't always going to look like cupcakes with heart-shaped sprinkles (or whatever it is you're picturing!). Love in your community is going to look like you being the most Christ-like that you can be.

I have a strange example about how love doesn't look like you might be thinking. Once in residency, I admitted a teenage boy with a chronic condition. It was late one night; he had been to the hospital over a dozen times before—he knew the drill and the strict procedure—he had likely been in the hospital more than I had. He was a cool teen with a wild t-shirt and dark hair who looked like he was hiding a big personality behind his quiet obedience in that moment. He was unpacking and I stopped in to give him an exam. But a strange thing came over me as I started to give the plan. I lied. Not just a little lie, but a big fat, juicy joke of a crazy lie. I told him that normally he could eat dinner and go to sleep, but that tonight we were going to do a series of really painful procedures first, withhold dinner, and not let him sleep at all.

His eyes got big as plates as he started gasping, "Wait, what...? Why...? Painful...?"

I held my serious doctorly composure for another few seconds, and then burst into a huge smile.

"I'm just kidding, I'm sorry! The nurse is bringing dinner and there are no procedures. It's just a normal night." His friend with him burst into laughter as the teen just sat there watching me closely, trying to make sure.

He finally grinned, exclaiming, "That was so mean!" But for the rest of his hospitalization, when I would walk by his room, he would chuckle and gesture that he was watching me, remembering our introduction.

I totally admit—it was kind of mean. That's the worst joke I've ever played on a patient. But you know why I did it? I was looking for any excuse to make him smile. I was looking for an opportunity, so that instead of treating him like number 25/30 on my list of things to do that night (because he was!), he would feel like he was included in my circle of people that I enjoy, and pick on, and love. Now many kids might not have seen that as loving—but that teenage boy got it! And you know why I wanted to love on him? Because I knew the reason he had come to the hospital late that night—his mom had just died.

Normally, scheduled patients are admitted during the day. But we had learned that morning that this particular patient had to go to mom's funeral in the evening, and then would be admitted late that night. It crushed me to think that after that day of heartache, he was going to be locked in his room alone that night. So, I made something up—on the spot— something that might bring him a smile. The joke wasn't done in malice, or with a specific goal that he pick me for "favorite resident of the week," or anything like that! It was done in love. He clearly saw that, because he was drawn to it— and would seek me out the rest of his time there. Because everyone wants authentic community! Everyone wants to be more than just a number, or a coworker, or a patient. Everyone wants to be loved.

It's so easy to say, and it's not that we don't understand it—but it's so hard to actually do. How do you honor someone who is not honorable? How do you serve someone who doesn't know how to serve? How do you love someone that may hate you for it? The *only* way you can do it is by loving God and letting Him take care of the rest.

Step one is to love God—and *let Him teach you real love*. Jesus was the example of love— that didn't look like Him simply being nice and handing out sprinkled cupcakes.

> ❖ Love looked like Him revealing true love in action to the crowd who wanted to stone an adulterer—*forgiving someone who did wrong and giving mercy in spite of it.*

197

- ❖ Love looked like righteous indignation as Jesus turned over the tables of greedy money-changers in the temple—*refused to be part of something wrong and didn't let anyone else do so either.*

- ❖ Love looked like Him freeing multitudes of their sins, demons, and diseases— *refusing to let the devil take another portion of anyone's life.*

- ❖ Love looked like Him teaching and explaining God in a way everyone could understand—*not saving all the best information for himself or a chosen few.*

- ❖ Love looked like honest heartache at the loss of a good friend in Lazarus—*a real and honest response to the frailty and pain of life.*

- ❖ Love looked like Him questioning the religious institutions—*admitting it is not all about following rules, but a heart following God.*

- ❖ Love looked like Him choosing the disciples and many others to follow His footsteps—*entrusting His teachings to people who would not always get it perfect.*

- ❖ Love looked like Him turning water into wine, calming storms, and feeding thousands—*living in the unexpected, the generous, and the miraculous.*

- ❖ **Love looked like Him laying down His life on the cross—*giving Himself up to benefit everyone else.***

Love doesn't mean weak or boring or sweet or nice. Love means honest, wise, truthful, and real. And whether they ever admit it or not—your work needs a lot more of that type of love. In order for us to bring any transformation, we need to know it too.

So, our first step is to love God and to let Him define for us what love is and looks like in our particular context. Step two in love is to choose to forgive grievances that we are holding, or that others are holding against use. God forgave you. Now you have to forgive those who hurt you and keep forgiving them. They may continue to hurt you, let you down, and lie to you again. Not trying to be a downer, just trying to be real.

I had figured I would be automatically good at this. Being the "holier than thou" Christian that I was, I made up my mind that I would forgive whatever my non-Christian friends did to me. They didn't know any better anyway! They weren't living by my biblical standards, I just had to see their mistakes as accidents. But then when my Christian friends started mistreating me, all my holiness went out the window! They knew better! They were being sanctified by God—how could they? Then one day God used an old acquaintance to show me that I had actually done similar things to others... my anger diffused.

We have to learn to forgive. Forgive those who ask. Forgive those who don't. Forgive not only our family and our friends, but also our coworkers and our enemies.

Love does not exist if it is only given for perfection.

Choose to forgive like God forgave you.

Step three is forget. Let it go (insert energetic Disney anthem here)! Stop thinking and reliving whatever happened—*how you got passed over... how you were the better choice... how you should've been acknowledged*—let it go. Then next week—let it go. Then next time they do it— let it go again. When it randomly pops into your memory a year from now—well, you get the picture. Just a reminder—you can't do it alone. "We judge ourselves by what we intend, but judge others by what they do." You have to learn to stop assuming the worst about people! You can't let the past determine where you are going—relationally, spiritually, or professionally. Love forgives and forgets. Love doesn't look like we expect it to. And love— unlike hard work, or perfect test scores, or great resumes, or fun ideas—has a God-given power that changes the atmosphere, surprises those around you, and rewards in its own way.

Lastly, the real goal is not to try harder to love people, but to love God. This whole book fits underneath this heading. Love God first, and all these things shall be added unto you—not only in your Christian walk, but also in your relationships, in your careers, and as you walk out your dreams. Love His heart, His goals, His plans. Trust him and believe! He's not the evil boss, ready to ax you at the first indiscretion, and giving accreditation indiscriminately wherever he feels like. He's not an angry taskmaster. He is not insecure or unwise or untrustworthy, that He would change His mind. He is God, the Alpha and the Omega, Who was, and is, and is to come.

He is faithful. He is truth. He is living. He is confident. He is wise. He is giving. He is perfect. He is grace. He is strong. He is glorified. He is everlasting. He is unchanging. He is family. He is friend. He is peace. And that's not even all! He creates. He speaks. He radiates. He reigns. He atones. He calls. He offers. He heals. He helps. He provides. He loves. He saves. He sacrifices. He gives. He imparts. And He makes incredible plans to involve us. He does so because He loves us. And He loves you.

A Conclusion of Conquering Love

"Therefore, my beloved brothers, be steadfast, immovable,
always abounding in the work of the Lord,
knowing that in the Lord your labor is not in vain."
~1 Corinthians 15:58

Now you've reached the end of the book and you are like—great, got it, I'm ready to go! Right? You are putting it all together and realizing that I instructed you how to be a full-time professional, and also gave you tools to do it like you're a full-time minister. I required you to know how to disciple as well as to evangelize. I yelled at you for lordship issues I just plain assumed you had. I instructed you that legacy was also required, and that if you were just spending all of your time doing exactly what I said to do for yourself, you were still failing if you didn't help others build too, right? I instructed, corrected, required, re-required, and asked a ton of quite impossible things in this book, if you think about it. And unlike most books along this line, I didn't end with the testimony of *how I did all the right steps and ended up as a millionaire, and now I'm going to share these secrets with you for just $19.99!*

Many people who write books wait until the pinnacle of their career and share their successes. I've done the complete opposite—and waited for a lull in mine, in order to share my failures—but I did that because more than anything—I want you to succeed!

I didn't want to write a book about how you should become just like me. I wanted to focus a book on all the things in my career that sounded perfectly Christian, but actually took me even farther away from God, so that you could learn from my mistakes. I've concentrated on my weaknesses and my battles, so that you will see, and hopefully identify with them. I'm still on my journey, but I decided to go ahead and share the bit I have learned...so it may be relevant to your life right now as you travel.

I want to end this book by talking about the movie *Wreck-It Ralph* and how it can be an analogy for our lives. I know it sounds crazy, but just bear with me—I promise I have a point. If you haven't seen it, Ralph is a character in an arcade game who is cast a villain, but he wants to be a hero. He hates his life—all he does it get put down all day for doing his job, which is to literally destroy things. Then, because he's the bad guy, he spends all his nights alone, wishing everyone didn't hate him. One day, he sets his sight on proving that he really has worth—that he's really not just a "bad guy," so he leaves his job to find a medal and prove himself. But problems soon arise, because Ralph has enormous, muscular arms, and monstrous big hands, and he breaks everything he tries to touch! He spends the rest of the movie trying to figure out whether he should keep trying to do something he is no good at, or go back to the life that he hates.

Now *Wreck-It Ralph* is a fun movie, but I also believe his story can be an analogy of what we try to do in our natural lives—fight in our own strength—especially in the workplace, where we know how to get things done. I saw this movie right as I was finishing my residency in pediatrics. That time was very challenging for me, because I had meningitis. I spent the first two years of residency living and working with symptoms of a concussion. I specifically remember the day I gave a concussion score sheet to a young girl who had just been hit in the head with a soccer ball. I had a worse score on the checklist than she did. She was instructed to go home, refrain from all activities and rest until her symptoms faded. But I was on call at the hospital that night and scheduled to work all weekend.

I very quickly reached a point in residency where I didn't have any more determination left. Working hard had gotten me through college. Working hard and figuring out new ways to study, and new time management techniques had gotten me through medical school. Working harder was all I had ever known or ever needed. But this time, I realized that no amount of "working harder" was going to change my situation.

But the ultimate goal for a Christ-follower is found in Romans 8:35-37.

"Who shall separate us from the love of Christ? Shall tribulation, or distress, or persecution, or famine, or nakedness, or danger, or sword? As it is written, 'For your sake we are being killed all the day long; we are regarded as sheep to be slaughtered.' No, in all these things we are more than conquerors through him who loved us."

Romans says in all tough situations we are "more than conquerors." Conquer means to "defeat or overcome by physical, mental, or moral force." That is what I tried to do—snap my life back into shape by sheer will. When that didn't work, I prayed for God to come in and "conquer," hoping for a moment of healing that would fix everything. But that moment of complete healing never came. When I finally got to the end of my training, *I had to make a decision to stay or go. I had trained in medicine for years, so it was either going to find a job I knew nothing about—or stay in this job I was starting to hate. I felt just like Ralph in the movie—torn between what I was capable of, and what I thought I wanted out of life.*

So, I started praying, "God what do you want me to do? Should I stay or should I go? What do I do?"

His very simple and honest reply was, "I love you."

I kept thinking, "Right, that's nice. But God, I don't think you heard me right... You probably just misunderstood—it's okay. What do you want me **to do**?"

But for three years straight, every time I asked, the answer was always the same, "I love you." It wasn't the answer I wanted, but it was the answer I needed.

I think sometimes we miss the pure importance of love. We want to go straight to the "conquer" part of the verse! But love is really all we need to know—which is why Paul emphasizes it so strongly. The word used here in Greek is *agapaó*, the same word used to show God's love for Jesus. This is a deep and constant love. Absolutely nothing we come up against can separate us from Christ's love, because His love is not predicated on anything we do, but on the nature of God. God loves us—no matter what.

In *Wreck-It Ralph*, Ralph runs around the whole time trying prove himself. He even meets a girl that he tries to help, but just makes everything worse for her because he is trying so hard to do things he wasn't created to do. What struck me most was when he said, "I don't need a medal to tell me I'm a good guy, because if that little kid likes me, how bad can I be?" All he needed was to determine his own worth. Finally, I understood, *my real issue wasn't the job or the illness—it all came down to this: where was my worth—was it really in Christ's love for me—or in my own ability?* I knew the truth for me.

Even being "more than a conqueror" is not something we can achieve by our work. Christ's way of conquering was not to take up a sword and fight or put on His thinking cap and strategize; it was love that lead him to lay down His life in submission to God's will, and in that simple act, conquer everything. Being "more than a conqueror" is what Jesus did on the cross. He didn't just make it through, *he triumphed—* over sin, over death, over everything that would try to stand up and get between us and Christ's love.

He conquered, and then left us with the Holy Spirit to help us do the same. *If He can conquer death, then there is no huge problem, no workplace environment, no awful coworker, and no corrupt system where He cannot use you to bring redemption into the broken world.* Once we come into relationship with Him, we can trust the best business partner in the world to change what was our heartache into our biggest possibility.

God has an amazing calling for you. There are probably going to be days where you may totally hate it, where you can't see the end, and can't even figure out what to do next. There will be moments of doubt, trials, and days when you won't know how to deal—but I hope you'll learn from me... and from Ralph.

Don't try to be someone you weren't designed to be.

I hope my story has showed you that *who God is calling* **me** *to be is someone who is calling* **you** *to another level of work excellence.* God didn't call me to live my life becoming the outstanding doctor of the year—the physician who gets awards; or writes articles that changes the practice of medicine; or incredibly mentors every coworker and student around me. Maybe He has called you there.

In sending me to medical school, God was not calling me to be a pastor—a full time minister recounting testimonies of life-changing miracles; preaching faith everywhere I go; and seeing lives changed in the community I serve every day. Maybe He has called you there.

God was calling me to live actively *in between the lines* of medicine and ministry, however faint they may be. I was not called to be earth-shatteringly impressive on one side or the other, I was called to walk the invisible lines, and break the boundaries that exist between the two. I was called to remind you who God is, what He is capable of, not just at church, but also in the workplace where you exist every day. I was called to give you a hope and a vision and a possibility for more than I can even do myself. This is His calling for me right now at this time in my life. It probably will change as I grow and move into other stages of life. But I am staying true to what He is calling me to do now.

As you go forward, make sure you depend on God, not on those strengths and abilities he gave you. You are not what you do, you are His child. If you can keep Him first place in your life, your work will be an enjoyment, not just a requirement. He loves us, He has His best planned for us. Even when things don't work out the way we think they should, He will bless us with the victory we need.

I am praying that you walk away reading *in between the lines*. I'm praying that you follow God into the greatness He has planned for you. I'm praying that you can benefit from my honesty and time writing this book—so that you can walk down the paths I have already paved.

I'm praying that you are the light that can carry these lessons on into the natural world—bearing both incredible testimonies and marketplace success. And I believe with all my heart that you will.

Walking out your calling is not a particular set of steps. It is a lifetime of small decisions. Some of which are obvious and easy to discern, and others of are hidden somewhere *in between the lines*. Trust God to help you master it, and do not be afraid to walk out life *in between the lines of faith and work*.

So, what is it that God has called you to?

Can you see your destiny clearly laid out before you? Or maybe you have glimpses of what you hope will come to pass? Maybe you only know where God has you in this moment, and are waiting expectantly for the next step of your life to come into view? Either way, God has called you to greatness.

God calls us to more than we can dream; once we begin walking and trusting in Him, He can take the smallest divots of time, energy, dedication, or talent we give and explode them into miracles of power. God has a plan perfectly engineered for you in your life, both in this moment and in those to come. Don't get discouraged. Don't give up. Great is your reward, not only in heaven, but also every day that you wake up and say- *forget the unknown, forget the fear, forget the struggle, forget the limitations, forget the past!*

God help me, and make me into who You've called me to be.

Notes

Lord of All

1) Quotation from Banning Liebscher:
   Liebscher, Banning. "Release the Supernatural". Q Conference.
   Nashville. April 2017. Lecture.
2) Lordship.
   Broocks, Rice & Murrell, Steve. *The Purple Book: Biblical
   Foundations for Building Strong Disciples*. (Grand Rapids:
   Zondervan, 2004) 21-30.
3) Royalty.
   Johnson, Bill & Vallotton, Kris. *Supernatural Ways of Royalty*
   (Shippensburg: Destiny Image Publishers, 2017).
4) Concepts *(including quotation)* from:
   Grudem, Wayne. *Systematic Theology: An Introduction to
   Biblical Theology* (Grand Rapids: Zondervan, 1994.)

Mission of God

1) Quotation from Sam Aiyedogbon:
   Broocks, Rice. *God's Not Dead: Evidence for God in an Age of
   Uncertainty* (Thomas Nelson, 2013) 212.
2) Quotation:
   Penn, William. Brainy Quote.
   https://www.brainyquote.com/quotes/william_penn_389538.
   05/02/2016.
3) Bible study class.
   Fidler, Bruce. *Metanarrative of Redemption* (Bruce Fidler—
   Ministry, Theology, Church, Hermeneutics, Blogger).
   fidworks.blogspot.com. 02 Jan 2013.
4) Relationships broken.
   Keller, Timothy. *Walking with God through Pain and Suffering*
   (New York: Penguin Random House LLC, 2013) 114.
5) Movie.
   Sister Act. Dir. Emile Ardolino. Perf. Whoopi Goldberg. Walt
   Disney Studios Motion Pictures, 1992. DVD.

6) Concepts from:
Keller, Timothy. *Every Good Endeavor* (New York: Penguin Random House, LLC, 2012).

7) Keller, Timothy. *The Meaning of Marriage* (New York: Dutton, 2011).

8) Middleton, Richard J. *New Heaven and a New Earth* (Grand Rapids: Baker Academic, 2014).

Power Shortage

1) Quotation from Booker T. Washington (quote found online): Washington, Booker T. https://www.goodreads.com/quotes/3189-i-have-learned-that-success-is-to-be-measured-not. 2 May 2017.

2) Quotation from Priscilla Shirer: https://m.facebook.com/ChristianPost.Intl/posts/10155631075993635

3) Audition.
Martinez, Cristina. "Schyler Colton Dixon Auditions." Online video clip. YouTube, 5 Nov 2005. Web. 11 Nov 2016. <https://www.youtube.com/watch?v=QM-K3NseVvE>

4) Sermon.
Laffoon, Jim. "Power Shortage." Campus Harvest. Kings Park International Church, Durham, NC. 23 March 2005. Lecture.

5) Quote. Laffoon, Jim- As above.

6) Holy Spirit gifts. Houston, David. "Pneumatology." Every Nation Leadership Institute. Bethel World Outreach Church, Nashville. 10 Oct 2015. Lecture.

7) Quote. Laffoon, Jim- As above.

Church of God

1) Quote.
Broocks, Rice. "The Proclamation: The Gift of Truth." Bethel World Outreach Church, Nashville. 18 Dec 2016. Sermon.

2) Matthew 14:13-21.

3) 1 Samuel 14.

4) Unchanged.

Marty, Martin E. *The Christian World: A Global History*
(New York: Modern Library, 2007).

5) Muscles.
Brand, Paul & Yancey, Philip. *Fearfully and Wonderfully
Made* (Grand Rapids: Zondervan, 1980) 167-173.

6) Extreme.
Marty, Martin E. *The Christian World: A Global History*
(New York: Modern Library, 2007).

7) Sliver.
Barker, Paul. "Church History." School of Campus Ministry.
Every Nation, Nashville. 15 Jun 2013. Lecture.

8) Concepts from:
Stark, Rodney. *The Rise of Christianity: How the Obscure,
Marginal Jesus Movement Became the Dominant Force in
the Western World in a Few Centuries* (Princeton: Harper
Collins, 1996).

Myth of Maturity

1) Quotations from Steve Murrell and Rick Warren in:
Murrell, Steve. *Wikichurch: Making Discipleship Engaging,
Empowering, and Viral.* (Lake Mary: Charisma House Book
Group, 2011).

2) Tomczak, Larry. *Divine Appointments: Igniting Your
Passion to Fulfill Your Destiny* (Shippensburg: Zondervan,
1998).

3) Chapter named after and Concepts from:
Murrell, Steve. *Wikichurch: Making Discipleship Engaging,
Empowering, and Viral* (Lake Mary: Charisma House Book
Group, 2011) 129-152.

Just Stop it

1) Psychologist.
Mitchell, Greg W. "Life Change Seminar." School of Campus
Ministry. Every Nation, Nashville. 15 Jun 2013. Lecture.

2) Avengers.
Marvel's Avengers: Age of Ultron. Dir. Joss Whedon. Perf.
Robert Downey Jr., Chris Evans, Mark Ruffalo, Chris

Hemsworth, Scarlett Johansson, Jeremy Renner, Tom Hiddleston, and Samuel L Jackson. Paramount Pictures, 2015. DVD.

3) Similar concepts from:
Weaver, Joanna. *Having a Mary Spirit: Allowing God to Change Us from the Inside Out* (Colorado Springs: WaterBrook Press, 2006).

4) Chapter based on:
Barker, Paul. "Inside-Out Transformation." School of Campus Ministry. Every Nation, Nashville. 1 Jun 2013. Lecture.

True Success

1) Quotation from Chip Ingram:
Ingram, Chip R. "Make Great Sacrifices." *Living on the Edge.* Producer Living on the Edge. Dir. Unlisted. Bott Radio Network. 2 May 2017. Radio.

2) Quotation from Booker T. Washington:
Washington, Booker T. *A Will to Be Free* (Simon and Schuster, Feb 18, 2013).

3) *Something the Lord Made.* Dir. Joseph Sargent. Perf. Alan Rickman, Yaslinn Bey (Mos Def). HBO. 2004. DVD.

4) History.
John's Hopkins Medical Archives. "That First Operation." *The Blue Baby Operation.* John's Hopkins Medical Archives. 15 Dec 2016.
<http://www.medicalarchives.jhmi.edu/firstor.htm>

5) Moses — Exodus 2:12, 3:11-15. Numbers 14:11-24.

6) Sarah — Genesis 18:12-14, 21:2.

7) David temple — 1 Chronicles 17:1-5, 11-15; 22:1-16.

8) Job — Job 1:1, 8-12.

9) Jesus — Isaiah 9:2-7, 53:5.

10) Proverbs 3:5-6.

11) Houston, Jonathan. "Are We Nice or Are We New?" Young Professionals. Southpoint Community Church, 2015. Sermon. <http://www.southpointcc.com/yps>

12) Tipton, Gregg. "It's time to shine." Every Nation Staff Summit. 8 Dec 2015. Sermon.

Releasing Kings

1) Quotation from Craig Groeschel:
   Groeschel, Craig.
   https://www.goodreads.com/quotes/852777-as-you-ll-recall-what-you-believe-about-who-you. May 2, 2017.
2) Title and Concepts from:
   Garfield, John & Eberle, Harold. *Releasing Kings for Ministry in the Marketplace* (Yakima: Worldcast Publishing, 2004).
3) Influence.
   Maxwell, John. *360 Leader: Developing Your Influence from Anywhere in the Organization* (Nashville: Thomas Nelson, 2005).
4) Nehemiah 6:15
5) Garfield, John & Eberle, Harold. *Releasing Kings for Ministry in the Marketplace* (Yakima: Worldcast Publishing, 2004).
6) Gnosticism.
   Fidler, Bruce. *"Metanarrative of Redemption" Bruce Fidler Ministry, Theology, Church, Hermeneutics.* Blogger. fidworks.blogspot.com. 22 Jan. 2013.
7) 2 Timothy 1:11-14
8) Broocks, Rice. "The God Test" The God Test. Engage Resources, 2013. 25 Jun 2013.
   <http://www.thegodtest.org/>
9) "My Best Friend's Wedding Quotes." Quotes. IMDb. 1997. 15 Dec 2016. http://www.imdb.com/title/tt0119738/quotes
10) The Lancet. "See one, do one, teach one." Journal Articles. 07 June 2008. 28 Dec 2016.
    <http://www.thelancet.com/journals/lancet/article/PIIS014 0-6736(08)60818-1/fulltext.
11) Johnson, Bill & Vallotton, Kris. *The Supernatural Ways of Royalty* (Shippensburg: Destiny Image Publishers, Inc. 2006) 216.
12) Miller, Brian. "Evangelism." School of Campus Ministry. Every Nation, Nashville. 15 Jun 2013. Lecture.
13) Mueller, George. *Answers to Prayer* (B&H Publishing Group, 2017).

Doubts, Fears, and Apologetics

1) Quotation from Johnson/Valloton:
   Johnson, Bill & Vallotton, Kris. *The Supernatural Ways of Royalty* (Shippensburg: Destiny Image Publishers, Inc. 2006)
2) Quotation from G.K. Chesterton (found online, but also found in):
   https://www.brainyquote.com/quotes/gilbert_k_chesterton_10 2389. 2 May 2017.
3) Deuteronomy 6:16.
4) Murrell, Steve. *My first, Second, and Third Attempts at Parenting: Discovering the Heart of Parenting* (Minneapolis: Mill City Press, 2015) 191.
5) Brand, Paul & Yancey, Philip. *Fearfully and Wonderfully Made* (Grand Rapids: Zondervan, 1980) 95.
6) Ecclesiastes 10:4-6.
7) Chapter based on:
   Keller, Tim. *The Reason for God: Belief in an Age of Skepticism* (New York: Penguin, 2008).
8) Barker, Paul. "Handling Objections." School of Campus Ministry. Every Nation, Nashville. 15 Jun 2013. Lecture.
9) Miller, Brian. "Evangelism." School of Campus Ministry. Every Nation, Nashville. 15 Jun 2013. Lecture.

Practice of the Presence of God

1) Quotation.
   Keller, Timothy. *Every Good Endeavor* (New York: Penguin Random House, LLC, 2012).
2) Responsibilities.
   Fraser, Robert. *Marketplace Christianity* (Kansas City: New Grid Publishing, 2004).
3) Hybels, Bill. Global Leadership Summit. 2016.
4) Fraser, Robert. *Marketplace Christianity* (Kansas City: New Grid Publishing, 2004) 87-114.
5) ibid
6) Matthew 6:33.
7) Brother Lawrence. *The Practice of the Presence of God* (St Athanasius Press, 2014).
8) Matthew 8:23-27.

Imago Dei
1) Quotation by Chip Ingram:
   Ingram, Chip R. "Make Great Sacrifices." *Living on the Edge.*
   Producer Living on the Edge. Dir. Unlisted. Bott Radio Network.
   2 May 2017. Radio.
2) Quotation by Karl Valotten:
   Johnson, Bill & Vallotton, Kris. *The Supernatural Ways of
   Royalty* (Shippensburg: Destiny Image Publishers, Inc. 2006)
3) Quotation by Martha Graham:
   Graham, Martha. http://quotes.lipy.com/remember-that-you-
   are-unique. 1 May 2017.
4) Campus Harvest. Kings Park International Church, Durham. 23
   March 2005. Sermon series.
5) Extreme Ziplining in Monteverde, Costa Rica.
6) Abram and Sarai — Genesis 17:5, 15-16.
7) Saul — Acts 13:9.
8) Gideon — Judges 6:12-15.
9) Peter — Matthew 16:17-18.
10) Quote and Concepts from:
    Groeschel, Craig. *Altar Ego: Becoming Who God Says You Are*
    (Grand Rapids: Zondervan, 2013) 10.
11) Piper, John. "The Image of God." Desiring God. 1 March 1971. 11
    Nov 2014. <www.desiringgod.org/articles/the-image-of-god>

Foundations
1) Quotation from Jossy Chacko:
   Chacko, Jossy. "Impart." Global Leadership Summit. Nashville,
   TN. 15 August 2017. Lecture.
2) Quotation from Jennifer Rothschild:
   Rothschild, Jennifer. *Lessons I Learned in the Dark* (Crown
   Publishing Group, Jun 24, 2009).
3) Broocks, Rice & Murrell, Steve. *The Purple Book—Biblical
   Foundations for Building Strong Disciples* (Grands Rapids:
   Zondervan, 2004).
4) Vince Gilligan creator. *Breaking Bad.* High Bridge Productions,
   Gran Via Productions, Sony Pictures Television and American
   Movie Classics, 2008. Netflix.

5) Chapter based on:
York, Kevin. "Code of Ethics." School of Campus Ministry. Every Nation, Nashville. 20 Jun 2013. Lecture.

Fear and Failure

1) Quotation from Tyler Cooper:
Cooper, Tyler. "When Failure is an Option." Medical Christian Fellowship. 11 Oct 2017. Lecture.
https://medicalchristianfellowship.org/
2) Quotation from Gist. Michael Anderson:
Maxwell, John. *Failing Forward: Turning Mistakes into Stepping Stones for Success.* (Nashville: Thomas Nelson, Inc. 2000).
3) Based on concepts from:
Maxwell, John. *Failing Forward: Turning Mistakes into Stepping Stones for Success.* (Nashville: Thomas Nelson, Inc. 2000).
4) Based on concepts from:
Cooper, Tyler. As above.

Why Work

1) Sayers, Dorothy. "Why Work." Dorothy Sayers. Essay. < http://tnl.org/wp-content/uploads/Why-Work-Dorothy-Sayers.pdf>
2) ibid
3) ibid
4) Concepts from:
Lyons, Gabe. *The Next Christians: The Good News about the end of Christian America.* (New York: Doubleday, 2010).
5) Concepts from:
Wallnau, Lance & Johnson, Bill. *Invading Babylon: The 7 Mountain Mandate* (Shippensburg: Destiny Image Fiction, 2013.)

How to Change the World

1) Quotation from Wayne Grudem:
   Grudem, Wayne A. *Bible Doctrine: Essential Teachings of the Christian Faith* (Zondervan, Oct 28, 2014).
2) Quotation from Francis Collins (found online, but also found in):
   Collins, Francis.
   http://www.explorefaith.org/speaking_collins.html. 2 May 2017.
3) Fidler, Bruce. "Metanarrative of Redemption." *Bruce Fidler— Ministry, Theology, Church, Hermeneutics.* Blogger. fidworks.blogspot.com. 02 Jan. 2013.
4) Garfield, John & Eberle, Harold. *Releasing Kings for Ministry in the Marketplace.* (Yakima: Worldcast Publishing, 2004) 71.

Teamwork as Legacy

1) Quotation from Melissa Spoelstra:
   Spoelstra, Melissa. *Joseph — Women's Bible Study Preview Book: The Journey to Forgiveness* (Abingdon Press, Aug 4, 2015).
2) Quotation from Walt Disney (found online, but also found in):
   Pugh, Tison & Aronstein, Susan. *The Disney Middle Ages* (Palgrave Macmillan, Nov 28, 2012).
3) Quotation from Rene Rochester (found online, but also found in):
   Rochester, Rene. *Models, Mentors, and Messages: Blueprints of Urban Ministry* (Zondervan, 2009).
4) Sierra Leone — information given word of mouth.
5) Inca's history — information given word of mouth.
6) CD Baby. "The Bourbon Family". CD Baby. 15 Jan 2011. 15 Jan 2011. https://store.cdbaby.com/cd/bourbonfamily

Beauty of the Mundane

1) Quotation from Raechel Myers:
   Myers, Raechel. "Daily Formation". Q Conference. Nashville. 15 April 2017. Lecture.
2) Abraham — Genesis 11-25.
3) 2 Timothy 4:7.

Independence vs. Love

1) Quotation from Timothy Keller:
   Keller, Timothy. *The Meaning of Marriage* (New York: Dutton, 2011).
2) Quotation from John Ruskin:
   Ruskin, John.
   https://www.brainyquote.com/quotes/john_ruskin_119951. 2 May 2017.
3) Niequist, Shauna. *Perfect over Present: Leaving Behind Frantic for a Simpler, More Soulful Way of Living* (Grand Rapids: Zondervan, 2016).
4) Bible says.
   Ecclesiates 4:9. Proverbs 27:17. Ephesians 4:32. 1 Corinthians 12:12-27.
5) 1 Peter 3:9.
6) Quote.
   Covey, Stephen R. & Merrill, Rebecca R. *The SPEED of Trust: The One Thing That Changes Everything* (Simon and Schuster, Feb 5, 2008).
7) Isaiah 9:6-7.

A Conclusion of Conquering Love

1) *Wreck-It-Ralph*. Dir. Rich Moore. Perf. John C Reilly, Sarah Silverman, Jack McBrayer, and Jane Lynch. Walt Disney Pictures, 2012. DVD.
2) Bible Study Tools. "Agapao." Bible Study Tools. Date unknown. 22 June 2013.
   https://www.biblestudytools.com/lexicons/greek/kjv/agapao.html

Acknowledgments

To my mom- none of this would have happened without you helping me think through the millions of decisions and hurdles involved in making this dream become a reality. Thanks for all your wisdom and patience at every single step.

To Miranda, Kristy, Rachel, and Alyssa—thanks for taking the time to look through the first draft of my book and encourage me on.

To Christy Haines, thank you for reading through my book as a favor which gave me enough of a reality check to get serious about it. Thanks for your prayers, encouragement, and honesty as an editor to help me get something that was clear and real.

To Marquicia, Jill, Naomi, Ali, Brittany, Nick, and Nicole—can't thank you enough for encouraging me to fight for my book even when I wanted to give up on it.

To my life group—thank you ladies for being awesome and being patient with me as I tried most of these lessons and stories out on you!

And last, but certainly not least—to the people who made this all possible—my **Kickstarter Supporters.** Can't thank you enough for putting your money and your faith in me to make this book a reality. You are all incredible people and it's been an honor to have you a part of the team! I hope this book encourages you as much as you have encouraged me over the last year.

Foundation *(Level 1)*

Terri Berry

Doug Bonds

Erin Burke

Alissa Brekken

Camille Brunson

Iris Ankrom-Crittenden

Sara Gill

Laura Hilty

Brittany Holmes

Elizabeth Lai

Kristen McCann

Rachel Mingus

Jay Montgomery

Karleena Olivier

Jillian Pope

Lesa Richardson

Rebecca De Los Santos

Jeri Shull

Evan Silverstein

Nupur Singh

Charity Spencer

Johanna D. Tweedy

Venneikia Williams

Legacy *(Level 2)*

Miranda Butler

Christy Marsh Haines

Roy Kiberenge

Bernard Payton

Lan Pich

Naomi Prashad

World Changer *(Level 3)*

Katie Briggs

Marquicia Pierce

Cynthia Tauriac

Frank Zhao

About the Author

Dr. Ashley Tauriac has focused for the last ten years on teaching and studying concepts concerning faith at work. After finishing her medical training at Vanderbilt, she worked for several years part time as a pediatrician, and part time for her church, planning international medical mission trips. Currently, as a physician, she is filling the position of locum tenens around the country. When asked, she's from New Mexico, even though she has been living in Nashville, TN, for the last fifteen years. She loves movies, music, dancing, and encouraging friends to discover and grow in their God-given purpose.

Visit her online at www.ashleytauriac.com